To Walk in My Shoes

Saving Grace on a Less Traveled Road

Rudolph E. Willis

LOST~~
COAST
PRESS
Fort Bragg
California

To Walk in My Shoes: Saving Grace on a Less Traveled Road
Copyright © 2000 Rudolph E. Willis

Lost Coast Press
155 Cypress Street
Fort Bragg, CA 95437

Phone1-800-773-7782 •Fax1-707-964-7531 • lostcoast@cypresshouse.com

Publisher's Cataloging-in-Publication
(Provided by Quality Books, Inc.)

Willis, Rudolph E.
  To walk in my shoes : saving grace on a less traveled road / Rudolph E. Willis. -- 1st ed.
  p. cm.
  LCCN: 99-73218
  ISBN: 1-882897-34-X

  1. Willis, Rudolph E. 2. Oncologists--Missouri --St. Louis--Biology.   I. Title.

R154.W55A3 1999   616.99/4/0092
[B]   QBI99-804

Cover design by Charles Hathaway, Mendocino Graphics

Manufactured in the United States of America

For my mother, father, sisters and brothers
— and all of those like them. If I have told
my story to others in a way that they cannot forget, then I have given to you all that
I can give.

For my patients who, every day, remind me
of the true meaning of living.

And especially for my family, who still try
— every day — to understand.

Thanks to Maia Gregory, who first waited four years for me to keep my promise; and, unlike others, evaluated my fragile effort with a gentle hand.

A thanks to John Fremont, who immediately saw some value in my work. And a special thanks to D.W., who taught me early that writers sometimes just write words, but editors write books. I am a writer, but you are a writer's writer and an editor's editor.

Chapter One

I have spent more years than I care to admit trying to numb the pain my memories bring—my memories of Chicago. Even so, there are always fleeting glimpses of both the good and bad—my outstretched hand clinging to my mother's red, starch-stiffened skirt as she strode proudly and briskly past curious admirers of my single, braided pony-tail, a custom of my great-grandfather; the screeching white-walled wheels and monstrous metal grill of a black '55 Buick drowned out by my mother's terrified scream as the car skidded to a halt just feet from my head in the middle of Washington Boulevard; the amused, knowing look on the chubby, sweaty face of the man behind the counter at the liquor store when I came in to purchase a "Beppi" Cola for my mother; and the joyous giddiness in my stomach when my father would sweep me from the floor and press me tightly to his chest.

But these are just fleeting, momentary glimpses from a time before first grade, from a time when I could still draw some innocence from my young years.

There is a song lyric containing the words, "Pools of sorrow, waves of joy..." These words ring true for me. The joy always seemed to sweep across the surface, momentary and impossible to cling to, while the sorrow remained deep and unmoving, always present, always real.

While I manage to avoid some memories, others will not allow me that simple victory. Such are the memories of the night of December 24, 1957.

I do not recall exactly when, but sometime between my father's last days in the employ of the American Can Company and our move to 1810 Walnut street, my parents applied for General Relief at the Department of Public Aid.

I was too young to understand the significance of this decision. In my mind, General Relief somehow represented society's way of belatedly thanking my father for his efforts during the war and for the way it had overlooked and ignored his many talents since. I thought of it as society's way of saying, "Sorry we forgot about you after the war. But now, in your time of need, we're going to reach out to help you." I didn't understand that General Relief actually represented society's most subtle and cruel weapon in bringing my father down.

By feeding his children for him, General Relief denied my father the dignity every man deserves — the wherewithal to take care of his own.

Man surely does not live by bread alone. And for that bread which man requires to live to taste sweet, he must earn it with the labor of his hands and his mind.

My father continued to try. I saw him steel himself in the morning for another attempt to find gainful employment only to return in the late afternoon, drunk from cheap wine because he had been turned away once again.

I only began to realize the real cost of our General Relief checks after my mother snatched me from a roomful of relatives and stood me straight up before her in the kitchen.

"What did you tell them?"

I swallowed hard, knowing what I'd said but not knowing what was wrong. "I said.. I said we got some free money from the government, ma'am..."

Her eyes flashed. "That money ain't free, Rudy. It costs more on the dollar than you can ever know."

It might have, but it was a part of our lives off and on for thirty years. My parents seemed to take some solace and pride from the fact that the money we received was not Aid to Dependent Children but the subtlety was lost on me.

Worse still, my mother kept having babies. Things hadn't seemed so bad in the early '50s when my oldest sister, Bernitta, was born, but then Yvonne, Andrea and Kimberly came after her and things continued to get worse.

By the middle of December, 1957, my mother was expecting our seventh brother or sister.

Saving Grace on a Less Traveled Road

That winter, the winter of 1957, seemed unusually harsh — the bitter cold had been relentless, cutting through the layers of clothing we wore on our skinny bodies. As was always the case, the General Relief money had lasted only weeks; and so, in spite of the Christmas season, we began to lose services to our apartment. First the electricity went off. Then the gas.

"No sense in troubling ourselves about it," my father said, leading me through the alleys, vacant lots and railroad tracks near our apartment building as we scavenged for tin cans and scraps of metal, which we then hauled in a discarded grocery cart to a scrap metal dealer several miles away.

"It's cold," I told him.

"Complainin' ain't gonna make it any warmer," he said, shivering himself.

The few dollars we earned for our labor went to buy wood for the two black, pot-bellied stoves that we tried to keep going when the gas company reached the limits of its compassion. Whatever didn't go to wood went to kerosene for the two lamps we gingerly carried from room to room after the electric company shut off service.

There was nothing to be praised about this existence. It was hard and bitter. My parents were acutely aware of what they were not able to provide for their children, but they were helpless to do more.

Each of us children reacted in our own ways to the deprivation of our childhood. My older brother James, who was a naturally brooding soul to begin with, was pushed to the limit by the cold, dimly lit apartment and by the thought of another Christmas without gifts.

"Ain't right," he grumbled as he snapped the clothesline attached to the big, wooden sled we used to haul the red kerosene can to and from the Shell Gas Station over on Ashland Avenue.

"What ain't right?" I asked as I walked alongside him.

"Nothing," he said sullenly. "Nothing ain't right." Then he raised his head and looked toward our father, several yards ahead of us. "How come we can't use some of the money for presents?" he called up ahead.

"We can't, that's why," my father said.

"We could do without kerosene for a few days. I could. We don't need to have so much kerosene . . ."

3

"We need the kerosene," my father said, not looking back at us.

Every time we made the trip back and forth, James and my father engaged in some form of this debate, with James' voice growing louder and angrier and my father's growing softer and more distant. Finally, my father seemed to duck his head beneath the layers of his frayed gray scarf — putting up a physical wall to match the emotional one he had already erected — and refused to respond to James' arguments.

I could feel James seething alongside me as his eyes burned ahead at the sight of our father, his head ducked into the scarf, his hands stuffed into the pockets of his dirty, gray overcoat. The cuffs of his baggy pants were shoved into the tops of rubber boots split open by broken zippers.

His very presence seemed to speak eloquently to his inability to satisfy the desires of his children.

"But it's Christmas!" James called out, his voice sounding flat in the cold air.

My father's shoulders flinched as if he'd been hit by a rock. But he didn't turn around and he didn't say a word.

I wish I could claim than I had an understanding of my father's silence, that I understood the pain he endured from the simple request for Christmas gifts. I wish I could claim that even in the sanctuary of my own heart I sided with him. But I did not.

Like James, I wanted Christmas presents and I did not consider the burden my father's inability to provide those presents must have been. James and I had long before outgrown the "presents" that we had been receiving for as long as we could remember — plain, brown paper bags with an apple, or a banana, or an orange. A peppermint candy cane. Perhaps a handful of pecans.

My mother carefully labeled each bag with our names written in bold, black letters, always with the very same crayon, the crayon she stored away the rest of the year so it would be available for that very purpose.

There were Christmases when our prayers were answered. One time, James and I each received a Mattel "Fanner-Fifty" gun, shipped from Los Angeles by an aunt who worked for the company. Apparently, our Christmas miracle was the result of mismanagement. Too many guns had been made that year and not enough holsters. As a result, James and I were able to spend the following summer running through the neighborhood playing cowboys and Indians, our Fanner-Fiftys stuffed down the fronts of our pants and between our legs.

I shared my brother's desire for a "real" Christmas. It was only our styles that differed. James was blatant, wrathful and determined to wreak revenge on the source of injustice — and anyone and anything might be held responsible.

But there were no miracles that Christmas. No special presents. What remains with me from that Christmas is the image of my father trudging in the snow ahead of us, goaded on by the taunting of my brother and my own silent acquiescence. And the events of the evening of December 24th.

James and I were different in a great many ways. While he was determined to confront the injustice of the world, I was a silent co-conspirator, secretly applauding him, guiltily enjoying his small victories and hoping for some benefit to trickle down to me.

So it was that I both fearfully and guiltily admired another of my brother's abilities which was beyond my ken — the ability to steal. At this, he was a master, a virtuoso.

As with all things done expertly, there is more than simple mechanical skill involved. There is the question of spirit and courage. Of attitude.

I never seemed to have the right mix of courage, adeptness and corruption to match his expertise in this endeavor, an endeavor that he excelled in effortlessly. As a result, I often relied on his generosity — not one of his best traits — after he had been on one of his sprees around the middle of the month, when we tended to run out of food.

Regardless of where he began his spree, he always ended it at the Shell Station where we purchased our kerosene.

So it was that day, as we trudged along after our father, that I could read the smirk on his face as masking his intentions. If Christmas was going to be greedy with us, it was clear that James intended to steal a little something back from Christmas.

When we pulled the sled up to the pumps, James let it slide forward and topple against the pumps.

"Hey now," the attendant said to us.

James shrugged his shoulders while I, characteristically, offered an apology. Then, without so much as a look back at me, James bumped against the attendant and then went into the station.

I glanced at the station as the attendant pumped the kerosene and I could see James' silhouette through the window, in the corner by the tall rack of potato chips. Suddenly, the face came close to the window. My eyes widened as James' head filled the panes full-faced, a roguish smile animating his features.

The trip back to the apartment was accomplished in silence, but as soon as we came to the foot of the stairs I turned and looked at him.

"You'd just as well give me that bag of potato chips now, James," I said, sounding like someone who believed he held a trump card. "If you don't, I will be forced to tell Mama about your stealing."

James paused and looked at me, giving me the same roguish, half-smile he had through the gas station window. Then he went up several stairs, lugging the sled after him.

"You hear me, James?"

He stopped. Although I couldn't see his face in the shadowy stairwell, I could hear him suck in his breath and hold it. I should have known what was coming.

I did not have time to react as the front of the sled slammed into my stomach and the back end crashed to the floor.

When the clatter silenced and I stood half-bent over and holding my stomach, James' voice came to me soft and nonchalant. "I don't got no chips and I don't got no idea what you're talking about, but I'll tell you what! You're sure on your way to getting your little butt kicked, I'll tell you that."

He picked up his end of the sled and, before starting up the stairs, shoved the front end into my stomach again. Once at the top of the stairs, he dropped the sled, pushed me aside and then stomped down the hall and into our bedroom, slamming the door after him.

I spent the evening whispering every conceivable threat into James' ear—to no avail.

"Look, if you expect to get anything out of life, then you better learn your ass to do something right so you might as well start with stealing. That or go hungry," he told me.

His advice may or may not have been sound. In either case, it didn't keep me from whispering to him long after we'd gotten into bed. Not that the potato chips were my only motivation. When I first learned that the rats in our apartment liked to gnaw on more than just furniture —namely, my finger—I had gotten into the habit of trying to keep James awake at night so he could keep me out of any trouble with the rats.

I did this every night, but on this particular night I wished that I had left the danger of the rats well enough alone.

"You asleep, James?"

"Naw."

"So, you think we got anything special for Christmas?"

"Beats me."

"Know what I want?"

"Yeh, some diapers to pee in so you can stop wettin' the bed."

It was true, I did wet the bed. For a time, I convinced myself that James was urinating on me every night. My father said it was because I was lazy. My mother just got mad. It wasn't until I was seven years old that she stopped whipping me for wetting the bed.

Not that they didn't try to get me to stop in more reasonable ways. They tried everything — depriving me of water in the evening, waking me up every two hours, making me scrub the sheet every day on our tin washboard. Nothing worked.

Maybe I was just afraid of the dark and the small, gnawing sounds that filled our apartment at night.

In any case, James' response convinced me not to let him know what I really wanted that Christmas. Not that it mattered. We both knew that we would receive the same paper bags with our names on them, filled with the same piece of fruit, candy cane and nuts, accompanied by the promise for new clothes in the spring. Besides, I wasn't so much interested in Christmas gifts as I was in keeping him awake.

"Listen, James, Mr. Butler bought a whole box of pies and I know where they are." Mr. Butler was our landlord; he lived on the first floor and worked across the street at Dolly Madison.

James seemed indifferent. "I didn't see him bring nothin' in."

"That's 'cause you was in the room."

He propped himself up on his elbow and looked at me in the darkness of the room. "I don't believe you."

"I can show you," I promised.

"Go ahead then."

I got out of bed and turned up the wick on the kerosene lamp, causing the congregation of rats in the middle of the room to scatter for the floorboards.

"I don't believe you," James said again as I began to head for the door, but I could hear in his voice that he was losing some of his doubt. By the time I had the bedroom door half-open he was right behind me.

Slowly, carefully we groped our way toward the kitchen.

In the kerosene lamp's light, I could see that my mother had removed the pie box from where it had been, atop the wooden park bench that was our kitchen table.

"Damn," I whispered.

"I knew it," James whispered angrily.

"Shh."

We moved along the chairs, the counter and the pantry but I couldn't turn up the pie box.

"Come on," James said. "We ain't got all night. Besides, I'm getting cold."

"All right, all right," I said, impatient myself. I opened the door to the ice box and then slammed it again when I saw that it was completely empty. As the ice box rocked, something fell from the top of it and hit me in the head.

"What the. . . ?"

It was a bottle of Mogen David wine, placed on the ice box earlier by my mother. Someone had told her—several children ago—that a sip of wine would stay her contractions. Obviously, she had felt the need to do precisely that this Christmas Eve.

"Hey," James said, poking his face closer as I clutched the bottle,

8

"why don't we taste some?" Not waiting for my certain-to-be cautious reply, he swiped the bottle from my grasp and tried to pull the cork. "Dammit, how d' you get this thing out?" Frustrated, he gripped the cork with his teeth and pulled. Rather than remove the cork, he was successful in biting the top of it off. "Damn!" Then he rapped the bottle against the edge of the table. Suddenly, wine gushed everywhere.

"Now look whatcha did!"

He wasn't listening to me. He was already sipping the wine.

"Not bad," he said, extending the bottle toward me.

"No way."

"Come on."

I shook my head.

"Chicken," he said with a shrug of his shoulders. Then he turned the bottle upside down above his face and guzzled down several loud gulps. He wiped his mouth with the back of his hand and then let forth a strong belch before tilting the bottle in my direction.

This time I took it. With my first drink, I gulped down half the remaining wine. Several minutes later, the bottle was empty and we were both drunk. I tried to suck a bit more from the bottle; failing that, I casually tossed it on to the wine-soaked floor, showering glass across the kitchen.

"Dammit!" James shouted. "Mama's gonna beat your ass for sure now!"

I giggled in response.

We stumbled our way back along the dark hallway, bumping into each other and into the walls along the way. We tumbled back into the bedroom, with me stumbling forward and bringing us both down to the floor. "Damn you, Junior," I said. "Whatcha get in my way for?"

He didn't say anything for a minute, concerned with disentangling himself. When he had, he sat against the wall. "Boy, Rudy," he said, smacking his lips, "I got to tell you, those chips sho' was good."

My drunken joy soured immediately and I glared at my brother through bloodshot eyes. "What you say?"

"I said, those chips I had sho' was good."

"You lied to me!"

9

He shrugged his shoulders.

My anger burst forth. I lunged at him, missed, and came crashing down to the floor. He scooted along the floor and then up on to the bed, dodging my wild charges. I grabbed a pillow from the bed and flung it at him while he cowered by the window.

I missed him but hit the crate beside the bed, the one the kerosene lamp rested on. The lamp flew across the room and shattered against the wall in a fiery explosion. A moment later, the room ignited.

"Damn!" James shouted.

I sat on the floor, my mouth open, my body paralyzed by shock.

"Damn!"

James, of course, moved first. He shoved me aside, staggered forward and then fell to the floor. On all fours, he scampered and crawled toward the door. I don't recall moving.

The next thing I remember is landing next to him in a cloud of lung-searing smoke.

"Oh my God! Oh my God!"

I could hear my mother in the hallway, screaming at the top of her lungs. Then I scampered as fast as I could, trying to get to the door as the thick smoke filled the room. Just when I thought I would burst, someone grabbed one of my feet and jerked me across the floor and into the hallway.

"Oh my God! James! Someone, get some water! Get Mr. Butler! Lord have mercy!"

James didn't move. He lay dead drunk at the top of the stairs, laughing.

Mama rushed frantically up and down the hall, trying to douse the now-raging flames with sauce pans filled with water. My father hauled my sisters down to the snow-covered street and then pounded on Mr. Butler's door before running back up the stairs.

A moment later, Mr. Butler's voice joined the chorus of screams. "What the hell's going on here? Oh my . . . Jesus Christ!" He cried out as he stumbled up the stairs after my father.

The sound of sirens and the rumbling of two fire trucks soon filled the air.

Saving Grace on a Less Traveled Road

I sat in the middle of the street with my brother and my sisters, shivering and watching the firemen pull the long hoses from their fire trucks and race up the blazing stairwell. The water gushed back down, turning to ice before it ever reached the curb.

I'm sure it didn't take long to put out the fire; but to me, sitting there in the middle of the street, it seemed to take forever.

Before she was pushed from the apartment, my mother had grabbed her robe. I looked up and saw how it hung haphazardly from her tiny shoulders as she stood nearby, rocking back and forth. "Lord have mercy. Please . . ."

Suddenly, she stopped and slid to the ground. My father took his overcoat and placed it around her shivering shoulders.

I will never forget how helpless she looked, stooped in the snow with my father's worn, gray overcoat piled up around her shoulders. She looked more like a pile of used clothing waiting at the curb to be hauled away than a human being.

I saw her face tilt up toward my father and I saw her mouth the words, "It's time."

After they put her in the ambulance, I pressed my face against its foggy back window. "I'm sorry Mama," I said. "I'm so sorry."

Then I stepped away, fearful whether she would ever come back again.

And that is what I remember most about that Christmas Eve — standing in the middle of the street, still half-drunk, cold, afraid and guilty as the ambulance drew quietly away into the feathered snow.

Ronald was born a few hours later.

Chapter Two

I was born in Chicago's Cook County Hospital on October 11th, 1950. I was not the first born to my family and certainly not the last. James preceded me into this world by two years, two months and two days. Deuces wild, we used to say... then.

I was followed by Bernitta, Yvonne, Andrea, Kimberly, Ronald, Brian, Steven and Shinette.

It is true that the world does not promise much to any of us borne into it, but to the heart of a child the world *should* make such promises. So it was for my heart one cold winter morning while I searched frantically through the bare cabinet for something—anything—to eat. I turned to my mother, and with all the injustice of the world's failed promises welling within me, asked her, "Mama, why in the world did you have so many of us when you knew full well that you and Daddy could not take care of us?"

More than the look in her eyes—a look that I could not bear but for a moment—it was the way her fingers gripped tighter on the edge of the park bench that served as our kitchen table which stays with me still. That and the struggle of her voice to answer. "I love all of my children," she said with cold certainty. "And that alone is all that matters."

My mother did show us that love, but it was not always an easy love because too often it was given under the most trying of circumstances.

I think that a child's life is too often lived in terms of what "should" be. That is the innocence of children. It is only as we grow older, as we look back and see how those "shoulds" became "was nots," that we suffer so painfully.

Our task as adults is to somehow understand the indecent and often

12

unfair balance between those "shoulds" and those "was nots," so that we can move forward in a way that allows us to grow and find some semblance of grace.

Still, it is the "shoulds" that speak to us so cuttingly.

There "should" have been more music in my home. My mother had the loveliest voice imaginable, but she had ignored the recording contract a New York record company offered her, captivated by the beauty of her sixteen-year-old voice.

"Now what did I want to go to New York for?" she responded when I asked her if she regretted her decision to wait for my father's return from the war in the sanctuary of the small choir in a secluded Baptist church in rural Arkansas. "Big city like that. I was scared of cities like that."

She didn't mention that, after the war, she followed my father to Chicago, where she lived her next thirty years in poverty and want.

I do remember her singing when I was a very young child, but I do not now remember when her singing stopped. All I have now is the certainty that when it stopped, it stopped for good.

My mother might have been frightened of the big city; my father was anything but. He embraced the city—as did so many other thousands of Blacks from the South—with all his heart, believing that it was in the Northern cities that he would find his dreams.

He had been a good soldier, fighting courageously during the Second World War. He came home believing that his valor earned him an opportunity. Nothing more. He never asked for anything more.

He came to Chicago with his dreams and his saxophone. He was born, like my mother, with music in his soul and a haunting ability to bring that music into the world. As pure and beautiful as my mother's singing was, my father's saxophone was raucous and riveting. Powerful. It was moody. The sounds that he brought forth from his horn could make you laugh and make you cry.

With that saxophone, he was a magician. A shaman. A priest.

Sometimes, when my mother was tired and that faraway look would come upon her, I could ask her about my father's music and she would remember him as he was and not how he had become. "Your daddy," she would start out, a smile lifting the corners of her lips, "Your daddy played that thing so sweet that he could make the Devil himself dance."

I did well to simply listen to my mother then because the wrong question could take her out of her sweet reminisce and fill her with anger.

"Why'd Daddy stop playing?"

Her eyes would narrow, and rather than that faraway look, an immediate and present danger filled them. "Why'd your daddy stop playing that thing? Same reason everyone stops making music. They get tired. They get scared. They get beaten."

The first time she told me of my father being scared or beaten, it didn't ring true. He was a big man. And to me, his son, he was an unbeatably strong man. Much of his strength was derived from his silence, which in itself conjured up mystery and magic to me.

My father was a silent man, but as I came to understand, his silence was not reticence. His silence was multifaceted and even now there are aspects of his silence which, when I recall them, bring me back into his presence.

To be sure, his silence was sometimes nothing more than a paucity of words; sometimes it was the delayed response to a situation which demanded an immediate tirade; but just as often his silence would take the form of a knowing smile, or a concentrated stare at something that did not appear to be "there" to lesser eyes.

However, as difficult as these silences were for a young child to comprehend, there was one face to his silence which seemed at once completely present and completely unassailable, even to the youngster that I was. He would often sit alone, late at night in a darkened room, his head cradled in his hands, enveloped by total silence.

When I would see him at those times I would be overwhelmed by fear and mystery and a pain that was both palpable to me and unimaginable.

Silence was the only sanctuary he was able to carve out for himself in the world. For a time, his music provided him with that sanctuary; but long before I was old enough to comprehend the man my father was, his music had become a cruel sanctuary, a mocking sanctuary, one which gave no peace, but rather tormented him with the reality of dreams lost and hopes forever unfulfillable.

Although there was no music in my home, there was family. There was love. There was, in spite of the conditions of our lives, the innocence and joy of youth. But no music. That had been silenced long before my own loss of innocence.

Instead, there was my father's silence. His silence was his refuge, the wall he built around himself. And it never invited me or any of my brothers and sisters in. Not once can I recall him sitting in silence with one of us on his lap or with his arm draped over one of our shoulders. There was no way for us to breach the sanctity of his silence and he never offered an invitation to bring us in.

Often his silences followed an alcoholic binge, a binge that ended in my mother's violent rage against such binges, a binge always—always—preceded by another failed attempt at finding a job.

"What's the matter with you anyway?" my mother would shout. "You got no job. We got no money to pay for heat and you're buying wine! What's the matter with you?"

I don't know. I suppose I always wanted my father to rise up in some righteous indignation when my mother would challenge him like that. But he didn't. He simply retreated into his silence, leaving the rest of us behind.

There were times when my mother told stories which shed some light on my father's moody silence.

"It's his way," she would say. "His way of putting up with the hurt."

The Hurt. That was the term my mother generally used to describe the indignities of the world, the cruelties and the unfairness. Just the Hurt.

"He never got to know his own daddy," she explained. "His daddy walked out on your grandma just after your daddy was born."

"When was that, Mama?"

"Let me see now . . ." She closed her eyes, sorting all the facts. "I don't know the exact date. It was early fall, 1921. Maybe September. He was born in a small town in Ohio.

"Anyway, your daddy was hurt by his daddy leaving and when your grandma got remarried, he changed his name from Milton to Willis, giving up any claim to his original clan.

"Soon as they were married, Grandma's new husband packed your daddy and his older brother into a truck along with Grandma and headed off for the Mississippi basin.

"That's where I believe he found his silence—on the banks of the Mississippi. His music too." She closed her eyes and smiled, as if she could still hear the sweet music he could play then.

My father taught himself to play on a four-stringed electric guitar he discovered in a junkyard. In high school, he traded a drum set for his first alto sax. Along the way, he taught himself to read music.

He started his first band in high school. During the war, a time which was for him a time of optimism and hope, he made two records overseas.

For years, those records were kept in a special place in the closet where we lived. One day they were simply gone. Once, when I was a boy, my mother managed to find a record player so we could listen to how our father sounded. Through the scratched and warped noises, I heard a sound that seemed to come straight from Eden, pure and strong.

The war changed my father just as it changed the world. It gave him false hope. His experience during the war made him think that life would be different when he returned.

"I had a lot of time to think over there," he said one time when he was in the mood to share stories of the war. "'Cause of my asthma, I couldn't sleep inside of those tents. I ended up spending my nights outside the tent in the middle of a jungle with those monsoon rains coming down.

"I had to be real quiet then, real quiet because I could hear enemy fire not so far away. I kept real still too because I could hear the huge blue racer snakes slithering in the mud all around me. Could see their tracks in the morning light too. Sometimes those tracks would stop at one of my footprints and then pick up again on the other side," he'd add, winking at me to emphasize the danger.

"I wish I coulda gone to war," my brother James said.

My father shook his head. "No you don't. It wasn't all dreaming outside of tents." His voice grew quiet as he began to describe hand-to-hand combat. As he spoke, he would crouch in the middle of the room and act out his description. One. Two. Three. In a lightning flash he would swing forward, bashing the butt of an imaginary rifle against my head and then slashing around with the bayonet to finish the job.

I would stare at him wide-eyed, my heart pounding and my breathing heavy.

He wouldn't move. He would just stare with pinpoint concentration at some point no one else could see. Perhaps into the eyes of an enemy soldier who had received something more final than an imaginary attack.

The rows of medals that adorned his uniform and the stripes on the sleeves attested to his bravery. Before he was twenty-one years old, he had been made a Master Sergeant.

A Master.

During the war, he could fight and kill for his country; but after the war, he was hard-pressed to live in it. Once he was stripped of his hero's uniform, he had to stand naked before a more insidious enemy, a more brutal enemy, an enemy more skilled at destruction than any he'd come across overseas.

The first casualty to this enemy was his confidence. The second, his pride. Then his music.

All that was left was pain. The Hurt Mama referred to.

Even then, I could not condemn him for trying to anesthetize himself with alcohol. I wished it wasn't so. But it was so. He was my father, but he was only a man; and very few men are able to withstand such constant, unrelenting indignity.

And fewer heroes.

There were times of joy and hope. Perhaps they were all the more inhumane for being so brief. The summer and fall of 1956 was one such time. Our landlord, Mr. Butler, managed to get my father a job at the Dolly Madison pie factory across the street from our apartment.

Every day he went diligently to work, and every evening he returned home proud. He had been there some time when he was promised the next available position as a driver.

17

The mere possibility of temporary work that could turn into a real, steady job was enough to make my father euphoric. During these times of euphoria, I was able to witness the witty, brilliant, soft-spoken man who was my father.

Then, a few weeks later, I found him alone in the middle of the night, staring out the living room window. The Dolly Madison Company had decided to close down the pie factory.

Within a few days, the man I had come to love as my father was gone, replaced by the more familiar, watery-eyed drunk who staggered home and forced us to endure his long, moody silences.

This surely was the way it was with my father.

Then there were other events so emotional and so powerful that they created their own realities. When my father's older brother died in a freak accident—a jack gave way at his gas station, allowing two tons of cold metal to come down and crush his legs—my father remained stone sober for nearly three months after the funeral.

The friendships my father claimed were with others who understood the Hurt. My Uncle Robert was one such true friend to my father. Like my father, Uncle Robert turned to drink too often. Like my father, Uncle Robert squandered too many paychecks on his personal sanctuary.

My mother and her sister, my Aunt Bossie, were constantly at their wit's end trying to keep their households together. Uncle Robert, a kind and gentle soul when sober, turned into something demonic when drunk. Many times Aunt Bossie sought refuge in our apartment with Mama, her sister.

Such was the ebb and flow of our lives—drunkenness, silences, moments of graces, long stretches of pain. To my young mind, that was how it had always been and that was how it would always be.

I was wrong.

One balmy, summer evening, on a Chicago street corner, Uncle Robert raised such fear and terror in my aunt that she had no choice but to ward off his attack with a steak knife she'd taken from her own kitchen.

The thin blade of that knife poked a small hole in my uncle's chest and pierced his heart. As my aunt screamed for help, Uncle Robert collapsed to the dirty sidewalk and bled to death, long before the ambulance ever arrived.

"Rudy," my father said to me the following day, "would you walk with me down to the funeral home to say goodbye to Uncle Robert?"

But even in this gesture my father was defeated.

By the time we arrived at the funeral home, Uncle Robert's casket was gone, tossed onto a plane and flown down south to be buried by his people there.

My father maintained a stoic silence as he walked me back home. But after that, he disappeared for a week. And when he returned, he was sober again for nearly two months.

Aunt Bossie ended up at the Kankakee Mental Hospital west of Chicago, and her six children joined us before we moved into the Cabrini-Green projects.

Our Walnut Street apartment occupied the second floor of a two-story red brick building wedged between a factory wall and Ms. Nellie's squat, white frame house. Across the street, the Dolly Madison Bakery sprawled out the entire length of the block. From our living room window, I could see the overhead doors that led to the loading docks inside.

When we first moved to Walnut Street I really believed that somehow those apple pies, cinnamon rolls, chocolate cup cakes and oatmeal cookies would all be available to me. By the time I was eight years old, all that remained of that belief was the constant knot in my stomach.

Not that I wasn't still drawn to the Bakery. I remember one night late in July, creeping down to the street and peeping through one of the tiny, square windows that lined the top of each door of the bakery. Suddenly, something huge and dark slammed itself against the door, sending me flying back toward the street.

My heart was still pounding as I hurried back up the stairs to our apartment—only to find my mama there waiting for me, leather strap in hand.

My mother was a faithful believer in not "sparing the rod." For her, there was no discrepancy between a well-deserved beating and absolute love for her children. She was determined to keep us on the straight and narrow so that we could become what the "Lord" intended us to be.

Of course, we all brought to the task very different talents and personalities. James had an uncanny capacity for substituting unfulfilled desires with behavior that was often self-serving and almost as often ruthless.

When James managed the small victories that the world allowed, a small smirk would animate his lips, a smirk that seemed to tell the world that he didn't give a damn about no small victories anyway.

I was aware of this aspect of James' personality early; it both irritated and delighted me. Delighted me in that it spoke so clearly to his desire to overcome our beginnings. I was not able to speak so clearly then. I was not blessed with his courage, his brashness.

It was only that lack of courage which kept me from acting like him. Certainly no greater store of virtue.

That aspect of his personality was his shield and his sword, the part of his character that created in him the potential to survive the obstacles that life placed in his path.

Certainly it sustained his will and determination as he struggled to find a respectable goal after completing high school. It kept him strong—and alive—in the rice paddies of Vietnam. It protected him during his aimless efforts to make a decent living after the war. And it gave him the grace and vision to continue to prod me along in the struggles waiting for me later in life.

"You can do it. You can do it." He told me this in stance, word and deed. James brought to the task a strength that was unimaginable in me.

But like the money from General Relief, his strength did not come without a mighty price. He had to build a wall between himself and the cruelty of the world so thick and so unassailable that the slings and arrows of society would fall back, bent and blunted. But walls cut both ways and it is hard to grow and know joy behind such a wall.

I am no philosopher and do not know all these things. What I do know is that something happened to my brother by his sixteenth year, something which took from him his familiar grin and shattered that brashness which gave me such irritating joy when we were growing up.

My redeeming gift was not strength and it was not insight. It was, rather, the tendency to do things backwards, not at all, or long before anyone could have expected me to.

20

I seemed to see things that were not as obvious to others and then to act accordingly. So it was when I was three years old that I noticed something very strange and disturbing about my own two feet: whenever I tried to walk, my feet always seemed to be pointed in the wrong direction. They had the tendency to bump into each other instead of marching straight ahead in the direction I intended.

I did not focus on my own two feet though. Once I became aware of this situation, I began to study other people's feet and how they worked.

From my observations, I could see that everyone else's left foot seemed to have a distinct, natural curvature as did their right foot. Mine simply did not.

I concluded that the situation with my feet was intolerable and that it had to be addressed. I began by putting my shoes on the wrong foot but that created a situation even more ludicrous; my feet looked as if they were heading off at one hundred and eighty degrees from one another.

I essentially gave up walking for over a year, even as I continued to put my shoes on the wrong feet. In spite of the discomfort and the frustration, my feet finally began to get the message and behave in a more normal fashion. Unfortunately, from the time I first noticed the problem with my feet until the situation was resolved nearly four years passed, four years during which I only walked haltingly, and in my mother's words, "was unable to tell his right from his left."

However, I had no sooner started to walk correctly—and ease her fears about my innate abilities regarding left and right—than I turned her fears that I possessed some kind of learning disability into a terrifying certainty.

I stopped talking.

As it happened, the two events—my walking and talking—were actually closely related. My battle with my foot problems did more than simply hamper my mobility and my ability to get into trouble. It forced me to sit still for quite a while. For most three-year-olds, this situation would have been quite intolerable.

I was saved by my cousin's comic book collection. The reality of the colorful, caricatured antics of Archie's gang, the dazzling feats of Superman, and the crime-fighting of all sorts of superheroes completely engulfed my imagination.

I was so thoroughly engrossed by the world displayed in the comic books that I simply stopped involving myself in the daily chattering that mothers in general—and my mother in particular—have come to expect of their three-year-olds.

Troubled though she was, she grew to accept my lying on my belly on the living room floor, flipping through page after page of *Superman, Dick Tracy, Archie, Spider Man, The Flash* and *Batman.*

"I don't know," she would say wearily when my Aunt Lois and cousin Tommy would arrive, "he's got some kind of obsession with those comic books."

What she couldn't know was that, while the words in the comic books were whizzing through my head too quickly for me to be able to grasp their full meaning, I was being drawn along by the events they described—sometimes at a furious pace.

It wasn't long before the only thing capable of distracting me from the comic books in front of me was the arrival of a new batch. I think my cousin somehow grasped that I understood more in the comic books than just the colorful pictures, that somehow I was taking in the words as well.

I would digest a new addition in only a few minutes. Frustrated with my desire for more things to look at and to read, I began to browse through a few of my mother's discarded *Reader's Digests.* I did find some satisfaction in these for a while, but it wasn't until I came upon the *Webster's Dictionary* that I was finally able to appease the strange appetite I had somehow acquired.

The dictionary was my bridge from the written to the spoken word. However, it was a bridge strewn with dangers. When I finally ended my long silence, no one understood what I was saying. I had managed to incorporate a tremendous number of absolutely marvelous words into my thought process. Unfortunately, my four-year old vocal chords and mouth were unable to accommodate the multiple syllables of these words, mangling them in the process of articulating them.

I understood what I was saying, every utterance. Too often, my listener did not. Most of the time, the reaction to my proclamations was a stare and a whispered, "Rudy's needing some speech therapy when he starts school."

I didn't need speech therapy. I needed the mechanical means my maturing vocal chords would bring. And they did.

If the dictionary was my bridge to the spoken word then the encyclopedia was the castle where all the marvels of the world of knowledge seemed to be contained. I would skim its pages and stumble upon marvelous, wondrous curiosities—ideas and objects and concepts that had been hidden from me. The more I learned, the more I wanted to learn.

My appetite for knowledge was voracious—one which often got me into trouble.

It was not long after I had read a section in the encyclopedia about our five senses and how they work in concert, that I conceived of an experiment to prove the case.

I had noticed that cats always managed to land on their feet, no matter how furiously James tossed one from our second floor porch. To my mind, they either had exceptionally good eyesight or their paws simply knew the natural feel of the concrete two stories below.

My four-year old reasoning suggested that if a cat was deprived of one or the other of these capacities, things would not turn out so well. Once convinced of my reasoning, I thought I'd make the experiment simple.

I decided to deprive one neighborhood kitty of both.

I crammed his screeching, squirming body into a paper sack, tied it, and then pitched it over the railing.

The sack plunged to the concrete below like a piece of steel landing on a magnet. I rushed down to collect my "data". I believe I would have savored the success of my experiment a bit more if the results hadn't been quite so messy. That, and the fact that my mother had witnessed the whole thing.

"What are you, crazy?" she demanded frantically. "You killing cats now?"

It was not her yelling that caused me to cry for a week after I'd buried the cat by the side of the railroad tracks. It was that I had taken its life.

Still, my grief passed. My thirst for knowledge did not. My mother was now convinced that, in addition to a speech therapist, I was going to require psychiatric intervention. She was, as the saying goes, at her wit's end.

My next experiment pushed her a bit further toward the edge.

My mother loved goldfish. She would buy a couple every few months, plop them into a large pickle jar filled with water, and pamper them with fish food flakes. She would enjoy them until they would eventually and inevitably end up floating at the top of the jar with one unblinking eye staring at the ceiling.

It was this unblinking eye that captured my attention. With their eyes open like this, I was convinced that whatever else caused their demise, it had nothing to do with their capacity to see. So one day I tossed a handful of dirt into the fish jar and watched the muddy cloud descend upon the two frenzied carp inside.

My experiment was inconclusive; I was unable to see if they blinked due to the murkiness of the water. By the time I had scooped out enough dirt to see them, they were already floating on top of the water.

I thought my mother would assume that they had died just as they always did. I didn't reckon that she would take into account the inch of dirt that had settled at the bottom of the pickle jar.

I had once again taken a life, but my mother gave me no time to mourn. By the time she finished beating my behind it was the soreness of my rear end which kept me in tears.

Sore rear end notwithstanding, I had begun to develop my own salvation from the harshness of the world to which I was born. I was fascinated by the world as presented to me in books. Of course, I maintained my fascination with animals and their behavior. I just modified my behavior toward them — probably more for my behind's sake than for their well being.

My respect for the life of small creatures did not extend to the rats that roamed our apartment. It was not their size which caused me to dread and despise them. It was their savagery.

One night while I slept on a chair to make room for a cousin who was staying with us, I awoke to discover the skin of my middle finger gnawed off.

"Oh Lord," my mother screamed when she saw my fingers, "he'll get rabies!"

Even after the doctor's assurances, my mother continued to rant and rave about rabies. Of course, I didn't help matters by moping around the apartment, displaying the enormous gauze the doctor had wrapped around my finger as if it were a war wound.

I was spared from rabies but not from the very real fear of the sounds in the night. To me, my fear was justified. After all, why would rats stop after only one finger? Maybe fingers were the beginning of an acquired taste.

Other than serving as a constant reminder of the ugliness of poverty, I could think of no reason that roaches shared our apartment with us. They were not only ugly and dirty, but vexing as well. I could not understand their suicidal swarming into the pool of warm water my mother left in the bathroom sink every night so that each of us could bathe before bed.

Greater than my vexation, however, was my fascination with the vision of the roaches disappearing down the drain in a funnel of swirling water.

Why did the water go down that way, rather than straight down as gravity would dictate?

Once, while pondering this question, I filled the sink, drained it and refilled it over and over again. I don't know how many times I had done this before I became aware of a presence behind me. I turned and saw my mother leaning against the doorway, observing me. Her face was masked with worry and concern. When I looked at her she simply shook her head and then turned away.

I don't know when she finally assured herself that I was all right. I don't know if it was the fact that I had successfully fixed my feet or the realization that the reason no one could understand me was because they had never before used the mispronounced words I constantly flung their way.

She simply reckoned me to be strange and had a weary hope that I might outgrow my strangeness. Other than that, she had more than enough to contend with—an alcoholic husband and six other children.

In my quirky desire to *know* were the seeds of who I would become. But none of these things are ever certain. There are more obstacles and traps and sadness than any of us can imagine.

Chapter Three

Our Walnut Street apartment stood only a couple of miles west of Cabrini-Green, separated only by Douglas Park and the meandering roads that cut through it before spilling into Ogden Avenue.

The streets flow forward in my memory like a living, surging map. Ogden Avenue merges at the southeastern corner of Douglas Park, gathering to it Kedzi Avenue and other, lesser tributaries before flowing eastward, rushing above Halsted in its mesmeric tumble toward Lincoln Park. At its highest point, where Halsted intersects Division, its broad, serpentine lanes momentarily swerve southward, flowing in such a way as to bring into view the sixteen-story gray monoliths of Cabrini-Green.

Cabrini-Green. Cabrini-Green. Spoken softly it can be transformed. A prayer perhaps. A mantra.

I was a young child and I once felt glad for the families that moved into the projects. I felt nothing but joy when I learned that we too would be moving to Cabrini-Green.

Cabrini-Green. Hummed by my mother it could have been a hymn.

The reality was never so benign or filled with grace. Before I moved into Cabrini-Green, it had been only the singular grief of my own family that animated my heart. In the concrete of Cabrini-Green I would learn only too well that the anguish of my family was hardly singular.

660 North Division. Although still in the distance, its monstrous and unimaginative size thrusts it right up to Ogden's curving current. A flash of sunlight courses bright and brief, engulfed by the shadow of 1230 Berlin, whose stony presence extends the length of Ogden's descending lanes.

At the bottom of Ogden's descent lies the patch of green at Cabrini-

Saving Grace on a Less Traveled Road

Green—a four acre parcel of emerald, a namesake, which sprawls southward one block, ending across the street from 630 West Evergreen.

Our new home.

Late September, 1962. It is a snapshot to me. A black-and-white snapshot. Grainy. Creased at the corners. James and I are perched high atop our furniture, which is itself piled high in the trailer hauling us to Cabrini-Green.

It is a moment and we are above it all. We are in transition. There is hopefulness. The projects do not frighten me. They do not sadden me.

They fill me with joy.

I am a child still. In spite of deprivations of my childhood, I am a child. Innocent and hopeful. I have my family around me.

We are moving. Moving to a better place. To Cabrini-Green.

In my eyes there is hope. That much is clear from the photograph. And in that hope there is, as in all hope, a pure innocence.

The projects were well known to me even then. I had watched Henry Horner rise brick by brick from the earth only a few blocks from our Walnut Street apartment when I was only six years old — six years earlier.

Then came Cabrini. My life was divided by their presence. Six years before. Six years since.

An omen?

James and I had roamed the construction site of Henry Horner six years before. I remembered bouncing up and down on the wooden planks leading into the gaping tunnel, which became a breezeway soon afterward.

I remembered the fiery redness, the newness and cleanness of the bricks that masked Henry Horner's concrete frames.

I had been witness to the birth of that great monster and so, having witnessed its birth as only a child myself, I never feared it.

That may have been a mistake. For the embrace that Cabrini was about to offer was different.

Only a few years old by the time we arrived, Cabrini-Green was already the breeding ground for restless, troubled gatherings of little black boys—little black boys who had no way of knowing or articulat-

27

ing the simple fact that their individual anguish would multiply and spread exponentially when they gathered together.

If God requires only the faith of a mustard seed, mischief sometimes requires even less.

What were harmless, mischievous pranks would in a few short years' time become violent, deadly acts. The groups of black boys would soon become the gathering of gangs.

In Cabrini-Green, there was precious little "middle ground." For much of my time there, by luck and the grace of others, I managed to walk that ever-narrowing middle ground like a tightrope walker.

Many times I have wondered how I managed to *survive* Cabrini, let alone thrive intellectually. Sometimes I find reasons. Other times I simply continue to wonder.

Cabrini-Green was a dangerous place, and like all dangerous places, it was best to cling tight to faith in something.

We were joined by one other relative just after we moved to Cabrini-Green. Uncle Larry, my mother's baby brother, first came to us from St. Louis in the summer of 1957. He was just a teenager then and his arrival was determined by a local judge who had given him two options—us, or jail. Uncle Larry chose us.

He returned to St. Louis several times over the next few years only to come back to us in Chicago. Finally, in 1962, he came to stay.

It wasn't until many years later that I understood that he was not simply an "angry young man".

Uncle Larry's problems had started soon after he'd begun to complain about headaches—headaches which were dismissed as "the kind all little kids get". His constant behavior problems were dealt with by beatings. His attention difficulties were attributed to laziness.

Uncle Larry was very early on at the mercy of the St. Louis juvenile court system. That court system branded him incorrigible and aided him on his way to becoming another young black man, rootless and angry, without the chance to demonstrate his worth to society.

Over the years his behavior grew more bizarre. Once, locked in by the screen door, he jumped through the closed kitchen window. Strange, agitated behavior. Telltale behavior, for those with the knowledge to recognize such things.

The happiest times he knew were across from Cabrini-Green, on the baseball field in Stanton Park with James and me. There, he ran and caught and threw, alive in the innocence of the game.

But then he simply disappeared. One day. Two. Four days. A week.

In the middle of the second week of Uncle Larry's disappearance, my mother asked me to take a bus ride with her.

"Where we going?" I asked.

"To visit Uncle Larry," she said simply.

"Uncle Larry?" I asked excitedly. "You know where Uncle Larry is?"

She nodded her head slowly.

That afternoon I went with her to the Greyhound Bus Station, and as I did every Sunday for the next year, I accompanied my mother to the Mantino Mental Hospital to visit my uncle.

One hundred miles west of Chicago on Route 57, that gathering of

The Cabrini-Green sign proclaimed our world.

gray, rectangular buildings haunts me even now. The cinderblock room in which Uncle Larry lived was even more haunting. It reminded me of Cabrini-Green.

Not long after we were able to bring him home, Mama forced him to find a room in a nearby boarding house. The eleven of us—along with Aunt Bossie's children—were just too many. There wasn't room.

Uncle Larry's headaches continued to get worse. The only relief he knew was walking around the block with his head thrust back so his eyes were looking straight up at the sky. He became a familiar sight in the neighborhood, walking around like that. No one even paid any attention.

I did not look up when the door to my classroom opened. I heard the footsteps on the tiled floor, but I did not look up. Not until my teacher called out my name.

"Yes, ma'am?"

"Rudy, you need to go to the office," she said.

I looked at her curiously. I had not been paying attention but certainly I had done nothing wrong enough to justify being sent to the office. "But, ma'am . . ."

"Rudy, now," she said, her voice insistent.

I didn't pay any attention to the girl who led the way to the office and it wasn't until later that I realized that she would not make eye contact with me. As we walked through the hall, I didn't give any thought to her or make any connection between her arrival in my classroom and my being called out.

The principal was waiting for me in the office.

"We've got some bad news, son," he said, easing me into his office. There, with the door three-quarters of the way closed, he told me that my Uncle Larry had been shot in the head.

"Is he . . . ?" I started to ask.

"We don't know, son."

I was dismissed from school to go home. I alternated between walking and half-running, both anxious to get home and frightened to. When I got there, I found my father sitting on the steps inside the apartment, locked in silence, his head cradled in his hands.

The door to my mother's bedroom was shut, but from the other side I could hear a low, continual weeping.

For the next three hours I stood at my bedroom window and begged God not to let my Uncle Larry die. Just after sunset Henrotin Hospital called to say, in effect, that my pleas had been ineffective.

Two days later, my mother called me to her room. "Take this to the storefront funeral parlor on North Avenue," she said, handing me a neatly-folded brown paper bag. Inside was a white shirt, a pair of boxer shorts and a pair of black socks. "Give it to the undertaker there."

I walked the whole way, the shriek of the L-train overhead the only noise sufficient to drown out the sound of my tears.

How I feared going to that funeral. I didn't want to go. I had heard them talking. I heard them say how my uncle had died and that knowledge fueled an infinity of frightening images in my young imagination, images of exploding heads and blood-bathed faces.

In the end, though the undertaker hadn't been perfectly successful, he had shown a mighty skill. There was only a tiny depression in Uncle Larry's forehead. Nothing more. Just enough to draw my uncle's skin into a saddened, slightly worried expression.

He looked as if he was asleep. Yes, that was it. He was sleeping and was perturbed by some troubling dream. Nothing more.

"Wake up, uncle," I whispered to him. "Wake up so Mama can stop crying."

My mother's sobs filled the room. Her wails of anguish reverberated against the hard walls. I hated for her to be in such pain. I wanted nothing so much as for Uncle Larry to get up and stop his foolish pretending so my mama could stop hurting. "I can see you wanting to laugh," I told him. "I see it."

I was twelve then and I was still ignorant of the cruel realities of death. I did not know how much of my uncle's expression was due to rigor mortis rather than the undertaker's skill—rigor mortis which had set in during the time it took my mother to somehow come up with the few hundred dollars she needed to bury him properly.

Time and money. There was never enough of either. And never enough answers. According to the police, Uncle Larry had gone to the tavern around the corner from the projects where we lived and the tavern owner shot him. The tavern owner's story was that Uncle Larry had burst through the doors, throwing bottles and glasses at him. "I didn't have no choice but to shoot him," he concluded. "He mighta killed me if I didn't, comin' in all crazy like that."

But why did he have to shoot him in the head? And what was Uncle Larry so angry about that he would cause another man to take his life like that?

Mama went to the inquest to try and learn the answers to these questions and others, but she quickly came to understand that her questions would not be answered, that the men who determined the rightness and wrongness of my uncle's death did not consider her questions significant or his motivations relevant.

In their arrogance, they not only vanquished any hope of righteousness we might have found in my uncle's death but they also vanquished whatever last shreds of faith my mama had in the American system of justice.

"Bunch of people doing what they always do," she spat when she returned home. Then she waved away any of our questions about Uncle Larry and the proceedings. "No one there paid any mind to nothing important."

She sat down heavily. "I got to take a load off," she said softly. She was a pretty woman but her prettiness was lost that day. She shook her head. I could see by the blank look in her eyes that she'd lost faith that America had the capacity to recognize and affirm the God-given worth of a black man. I had witnessed that faith dying during my father's endless struggle to maintain his dignity and provide the basic necessities his family required. That afternoon I witnessed its final, uneasy resting.

At Uncle Larry's funeral, I witnessed the agony of her pain, without the benefit or comfort of a faith in justice to buffer it. In between sobs, she would stop pacing in front of my uncle's coffin to stare with those same blank eyes at the handful of people scattered here and there on the hard, cold pews. Her eyes would come to rest on my father, sitting alone in the back of the room, his head cradled in his large hands. She would hold her gaze on him, and even though he did not look up, his shoulders seemed to sag a little bit more. Then she would look away. She would scan the faces of my brothers and sisters and then, before returning to my uncle, she would look at me, searing into my consciousness the powerful alchemy of her anger and pain—along with an undying image of futility.

Perhaps that sense of futility, more than anger and pain, was why— even after I came to believe that Uncle Larry was not merely asleep, that he was really dead—I did not cry. Why I did not cry again for a long, long time.

While danger came from all directions at Cabrini, so did protection. Luckily for me my cousins, the Pruitts, had already made a name for our clan before our arrival. I didn't realize just how luckily until I was walking home from my sixth-grade class one day.

I came to a throng of gang-bangers blocking most of the sidewalk, posing in menacing nonchalance. In the same way that I had come to know not to show a growling dog fear, I knew to move along past such groups, looking straight ahead and keeping my posture non-threatening.

I was just about to turn the corner near my building when I had to step off the curb to stay clear of some of the bangers. My eyes were on my feet—my once turned feet—as they stepped down into the gutter.

I never saw the banger move toward me. I suddenly felt the grip at the back of my collar. I didn't have time to swallow before I was lifted up over the curb and slammed into the brick wall.

I bounced off the bricks only to feel his fist land hard against my stomach.

I felt the wind burst out of me as I crumpled down to the hard concrete of the sidewalk. Even without wind in my lungs, even without a defense, even then I knew to draw my legs in and curl down in a fetal position.

I could only wait for the real beating to begin.

There was no alternative. Even if I could somehow get up from the sidewalk and confront my attacker, the act of bravery would earn me little more than a bullet in the back of the head.

Courage and foolishness were synonymous in Cabrini-Green.

I was prepared for a beating. I was not willing to die, not if I could help it. I tried to remember everything James had told me about preparing myself for such an attack. My knees were up. My face down. My arms protected the front of my body. My sides and back were vulnerable to attack, but there was nothing I could do about that.

"And don't cry out," James told me. "Don't never cry out. Take the beating like a man. That way, they might respect you the next time."

How quickly these thoughts and others rushed through my twelve-year-old mind as I braced myself for an attack that did not come.

"Man, you crazy!" someone snapped at my attacker, pushing him aside. "Ain't that Pruitt's cousin?"

There was a brief pause in which I sensed my attacker and the others exchanging glances. Then, only the sound of footsteps as they bopped back down Clybourn before word could reach Apartment 602 at 1340 Larrabee.

Before I uncoiled myself I said a silent prayer to God for the presence of the Pruitts.

In the projects, protectors needed to be immediate.

When I told James about what happened, he just grunted. "Just watch your ass," he warned me. "One day someone'll come looking for you *because* you Pruitt's cousin."

"You think?" I asked him, suddenly less than thrilled by my protection.

"I don't think," he said. "I know."

A week. Two weeks. A month passed. My wariness at James' warning eased. I began to think that maybe I was okay. The sun was out one day and we were playing a pick-up game of baseball at the diamond in Stanton Park.

I was on the pitcher's mound when some young thug strutted himself out from 1230 Berlin and onto the diamond.

"Hey, we're playing a game here," James called from left field.

"I don't care what y'all are doing here," he said.

"Come on," the third baseman called. "Let us play."

"No one does nothin' unless I say to do it," the thug snapped. "This is my baseball diamond. This is my fucking park. You assholes got it?"

We glanced at each other, trying to decide what to make of this interruption. I shrugged out toward James. He waved to me as if to tell me to go ahead and pitch.

I turned and peered at the batter, who looked from me to the thug and back.

"Hey, I said you don't do shit here unless I tell you to." Then he raised himself up a bit and peered at me. "Hey, I know who you are, don't I? Yeah, you're that Pruitt cousin."

I stood on the mound, glaring at him.

"Let me tell you something," he threatened, glaring back. "I'm the baddest dude here. I run this place. And you're gonna do exactly what I tell you to do." With that, he pulled a switchblade from his pocket, hit the switch and then waved a gleaming, six inch blade in the sky. "Now, you got something to say about that?" he challenged me.

"You might as well use that fancy knife on yourself," I told him, keeping my voice firm. "Because if any great harm comes my way, my cousin will probably end up cutting you up and storing you in your own damned ice box anyway."

The thug laughed with everyone else when I said that, finding some ironic humor in my shrewd joke. Then he stood dead still, his knife in his hand, his eyes on me.

I did not waver. I knew that I was safe as long as I could keep my eyes on him. If he was going to cut me up, he was going to do that no matter what I said or did. I had to play out the hand I'd been dealt.

He continued to consider my words, trying to weigh whether they were bluff or truth. A moment later, he chuckled again and shook his head. "You're a crazy little fuck, you know that?" Then he snapped the knife shut and turned and walked away.

Stanton Park was the only patch of green at Cabrini-Green. Often my father would come and sit at night time on a bench beneath the streetlight.

35

I took a deep breath as I watched him leave to make his reputation someplace else.

"Hey, you gonna stand there all day or are you gonna pitch that ball?"

I turned and looked at James standing in shallow left field. He was grinning at me. I grinned back. He started to laugh. Then I started to laugh back. Soon we were both rolling on the field, laughing. Him in left field. Me on the dirt of the pitcher's mound.

We were alive and we were laughing. Summertime. Playing baseball. And we were alive.

The relief was overwhelming and joyous. I was not blind to the fact that only dumb luck and a quick mind—and those Pruitts—saved me from becoming just another statistic during my first couple of years at Cabrini.

But while my brother and I carved out our own destinies at Cabrini, trying not to become statistics, my father was well on his way to becoming a statistic himself.

After Uncle Robert and Uncle Larry died, my father found a new sanctuary beneath the tracks of the elevated train on North Avenue. There, he found a congregation of men like himself. Men broken by the harshness of the world. Men who, like my father, probably dreamed a little too much, hoped a little too much, cared a little too much.

There were other musicians, artists, and philosophers in that congregation of lost and broken souls.

There were no walls and there was no door, no altar and no pews, but that congregation was as surely a church as any church there ever was. There, the heavy-hearted, dispirited and dispossessed old black men who still felt the sting of their life prospects lost found relief in the numbness that alcohol offered.

There was nothing about seeing my father there that made me proud. Nothing that filled me with gratitude, or even love and sadness.

All I could say about it was that I always knew where to find my father in a time of crisis. I suppose few boys in Cabrini could have said the same.

Chapter Four

The Pruitts could provide protection for my body, but my soul was becoming more and more vulnerable. To find some solace and protection I turned to what was at once both the most likely and yet unlikely place, the Clybourn Missionary Baptist Church.

The church was little more than a renovated storefront—a small room with two large plate glass windows that had been partially blocked by walls of brick.

I had seen that church many Sunday mornings and I was always surprised that there was never a crowd of people pouring out of it on Sunday mornings like the other churches in the neighborhood. Instead there was a stream of neighborhood kids who ventured into that place twice a week. One of those kids was Forest Brown.

Forest was my friend. We met the first day I moved to Cabrini and we became best friends right away. We had a lot in common. Like me, he had a huge family. I never did figure out exactly how many brothers and sisters crowded into the Brown's small apartment. All I knew was that there were Browns everywhere.

Forest and I knew how to work our way amongst our large families. We both also stood apart from our families in that we were both prodigious readers and learners. He and I sat near each other in the sixth, seventh and eight grades. Although he seemed subdued in class, he was in fact startlingly brilliant.

When we took the scholastic achievement examination to win entrance to Lane Technical High School, I had no doubt that Forest would do exceedingly well. I worried about my own performance.

We shared the burden of poverty along with our other commonalties. Poverty weighed heavier on him than it did on me. Even so, it wasn't poverty that would ultimately shatter my best friend's boundless ability. Like all of us, Forest first had to play out the role of a child in a place where childhood didn't exist. And we all had to come face to face with who we were, and the merciless consequences.

Forest appeared in class a few days before summer vacation with a broad, toothy grin on his face.

"What you got that stupid smile on your face for?" I asked him.

"Cause I know something you don't," he said, teasing me along.

"Yeah, and what's that?"

"I know I'm going to summer camp this summer," he said, his voice so well contained that I wasn't sure I'd heard what I'd heard.

"What?"

"I'm going to summer camp this summer," he said, mouthing each word mockingly as though he was talking to someone hard of hearing.

I was shocked. Stunned. At Cabrini-Green going to summer camp was like spending a month at a fancy resort in Palm Springs. Maybe the French Riviera. Man, going to summer camp was beyond the dreams of most of the kids living at Cabrini.

The best they hoped for during the summer was the occasional broken fire hydrant.

I looked at him for a long time, trying to read something in his expression that would tell me that he was making it up. All I saw in his face was the honest truth.

"How come you get to go to camp?" I asked him.

"These three old white ladies—" he began.

"Hold it right there," I insisted. "Isn't it bad enough you're telling me tales about going to camp? Now you got to make up some story about three old white ladies? Who are they? The fairy godmothers?"

Forest laughed in the way Forest used to laugh, using his whole body. He laughed and laughed, showing his teeth, pressing his arms against his belly, rocking back and forth.

When he was finished, he wiped his eyes. "No, they ain't my fairy godmothers. Nothing like it. They're just these old white ladies who come to Clybourn Missionary Baptist Church every week to teach Bible verses to the kids at Cabrini.

"You should come on down. All you got to do to win a free trip to Camp Sunshine is to memorize a few verses."

And so I was convinced to get to the Clybourn Missionary Baptist Church—to get some religion and to win a trip to summer camp.

That summer was the first time in my life that I discovered that serenity, real serenity, existed in this world.

But that serenity was only an island in a vast sea of discontent and anguish. Summer camp was summer camp. Life was Cabrini. Those of us from Cabrini knew a world that others could not even imagine, a world in which poverty held us in a death grip, squeezing tighter and tighter whatever hope and life-blood might be coursing in our veins.

Those of us baptized in the reality of Cabrini learned early that squandering hope on a compassionate life was worse than a fool's game; it guaranteed the real horror of poverty's hold—the murderous, strangling grip of defeat.

The defeat that was the gift of Cabrini was like an heirloom, passed down through the generations. Once one of the fathers had it, it became a gift to the sons and to the sons' sons—unto the seventh generation, no doubt.

Poverty and defeat became as much a part of the heritage of the children of Cabrini as the color of their skin.

There was no need for graduate work in sociology or social work to understand this. Advanced education was not required. Matriculation on any level was optional at best. The lesson of Cabrini in all its cruel emanations was a lesson learned in the hearts and souls of the men and women who lived there, who knew Cabrini's streets.

My father knew it. He knew it and he railed against it with whatever thin shreds of dignity remaining in his heart. No, he did not raise his fists at the heavens. I'm afraid there is nothing that poetic about poverty and its relentless lesson of defeat.

My father railed against poverty's lesson by attempting to do the impossible. His was an heroic attempt, heroic because of its ultimate futility—futile because of its context in Cabrini. My father attempted with relentless determination to feed, clothe and provide shelter for his ten children.

The little church that helped me find peace.

He took whatever job that came along. Anything at any wage. He never argued for more money. To do so would have been to concede the job to any of the other hundreds of men willing to do the same for less.

I say that his futile attempt to be nothing more than a providing father to his children was heroic. That is only partly true. His motivation was his children on the one hand but on the other, he struggled against an unquenchable fear, a fear of ultimate failure.

In the face of this fear, pride was swallowed, dignity was overlooked, the mettle of a man was not questioned. His was a fear of finally crossing that final line when self-dignity was gone. When a man could no longer say, "I work for a living."

Beyond that, there was only blackness.

The lesson that my father knew did not take any of his children long to learn. Children are, after all, insatiable learners. That our classroom was Cabrini and our teacher was poverty did not change that fact.

Like our father, James and I made sure we never missed an opportunity that might result in pockets that jingled when we walked. Usually, the only opportunity we ever got was delivering newspapers. That was all fine and good, but James was never quite satisfied with "whatever we could get." James, with his roguish survival instincts, was always looking for a way to get a little more than that.

As a result, the two of us generally caught a fair amount of trouble.

This was particularly true one winter when James decided that the *Chicago Sun Times* wasn't paying us enough for what we were doing.

"Damn, here we are out here in the cold. My fingers're numb. I'm tired as hell."

"So? What'd you expect to do about it?" I asked him.

"Get a raise," he said.

"A raise? What are you, crazy?"

He smiled a smile that suggested that maybe he was, in fact, crazy. Then he continued to fling papers at our customers' doors.

"James, what're you thinking?"

He shrugged.

"James . . ."

I found out what he was thinking soon enough. He had worked out what he considered fair compensation for our winter, pre-dawn labors— every penny he had collected on the entire paper route.

The manager showed up a few hours later at our apartment. Crowding in the doorway behind him was ten other paperboys.

"Where's the money?" he said simply.

"What money?" James asked.

"Don't give me any of that crap. You collected money from your customers today and I haven't seen a penny of it."

Behind him, the other paperboys were looking mean and restless. James liked fair compensation but he was hardly stupid. He argued for a while just for the sake of arguing and then he handed over the money to the manager.

After the manager counted the money, he left with a look on his face that made it clear that there was really no point to showing up the following morning. Not James. Not me.

"I don't like their editorializing anyways," James said after he closed the door.

I was mad, but that cracked me up. That was just like James. Making me mad and then cracking me up. He didn't like their editorializing. Right.

Just like that guy in mythology who pushed the rock up the mountain only to have it roll back down so he was forced to start all over again, the newspaper setback did not hinder my own determination to do whatever I could during those years to lessen the sting of our poverty—even if my plans and determination didn't always work out.

The following summer I found a job working as a stock boy in a tiny grocery store on North Avenue. You'd have thought I was working in Fort Knox the way I took care of everything. That stock room was neat and tidy. The shelves were stocked with perfect rows of cans and bottles. The floors were mopped.

I was perfectly content working there. I liked working hard. Then the bubble burst. A shabbily dressed customer came into the store with a shopping bag neatly folded beneath his arm. He went up and down the aisles, putting groceries in the bag. When it was full, he walked out without bothering to pay for a single item.

The owner's son was furious over what had happened.

"What's the matter with you people?!" he shouted as he snatched a gun out of a drawer behind the checkout counter.

"Goddammit! Can't you do anything right?" He waved the gun in the air and then began stomping down one of the aisles, heading in my direction.

When he saw the milk bottle I was holding in my hand, he seemed to calm down. I didn't say a word. He stepped aside and watched me while he stood in the middle of the floor, the gun pressed tight against his pant leg.

I was quiet and thoughtful about what had happened. I didn't say a word about it, though, until several days later.

"You know," I mentioned to my mother, "the owner's son at the store is a weird guy."

"You've got no call to be calling anyone names," she said.

"Sure I do," I argued. Then I told her about what had happened that day.

Before I was finished, she was on her feet, livid. "How dare he talk to you like that!" she screamed. "And to show you a gun like that! He's not weird, he's dangerous. I'm going down there right now and . . ."

"No, Mama. I don't need you to go there for me."

She looked at me with fire in her eyes. "No one's drawing a gun on one of my children while I got breath in my lungs," she said, her eyes narrowed with determination.

"Just don't go to the store. I don't want you to."

Her rage quieted. "I don't want nothing bad to happen to you," she said in a whisper. "Not you."

It was only later, when I played out this scene with my mother over and over that I began to understand why she had reacted with such anger when I told her what had happened in the store.

She saw in me, even then, something special—something unique even among her own children—that could grow and show the world that something good could survive the worst that life had to offer.

She saw in me the answer to the fullness of life's indignity to her and our family. She saw in me the answer to the fact that she had buried her own baby brother only a few years earlier, shot dead in a tavern.

I was the one who would have to answer for everything and she wasn't about to sit idly by while I was threatened.

Like her singing voice, my mother's indignation was complex and multifaceted. It could rise to the height of angels or fall to the depths of despair. There was joy and sadness mixed together and pulled apart. My mother, in her heart and in her voice, could feel and express the entire spectrum of emotions on this earth.

My father's silence was just one of the many triggers that would cause her to erupt in uncontrolled anger and violence. His brooding, drunken silence ate away at any hope of serenity in our family, because it was such an unfailing witness against such serenity. This and his drinking represented only one of my mother's seemingly endless triggers.

She might fester like an ugly wound over being crossed. She might contain the roiling sea of her emotions. But this was the most dangerous of situations, because although its presence was unmarked save for the burning gaze of her eyes, it could burst forth in horrible torrents.

Before that point, her contained anger would throb within her, pounding in waves of high-pressured blood that gave her chronic headaches.

My mother was the receptacle of the emotions my father refused to express. She was burdened with the feelings that the slings and arrows of life had aimed so incredibly accurately at us.

Yes, she could sing with the angels but she could feel her feet held to the burning fires of hell—the reality of the life she had been given on this earth.

After we had moved to Cabrini, her emotional burdens became overwhelming. My father became an ever more determined congregant in the church of the damned beneath the el tracks. He numbed the pain with alcohol and drew in the walls that guarded his heart and soul so that they were contained in an ever shrinking and dark space.

My mother did battle without the benefit of alcohol and without the benefit of a society of failure. She defended her wellbeing against the stark realities of life at Cabrini. Her eyes were wide open and she saw and heard the horror that surrounded her and her family.

She never blinked.

Of the two of them—my father and my mother—I could never say who suffered more. They both shared the cruel knowledge that there was no way out for them.

James' way out would be along the jungle paths of Vietnam. By a quirk of fate and chronology, my way would be different.

One day my mother was called to the principal's office to discuss some of my test results.

"Rudy has always had a problem . . ." my mother began as she was ushered into the office. It was only after she had been seated and calmed down that the principal explained that the problem had to do with the test, not with me.

"The sixth grade test is designed to measure verbal ability," she explained to my mother. "However, there was some problem in assigning a score to Rudy's test . . ."

There was some discussion about statistical analysis and the techniques employed for measuring results. The bottom line was that I had tested beyond the upper end of the scale. They could not accurately measure my verbal ability.

"Gifted" was the term they used for me that day.

That day stands out for me because it was only that day among all the days of my childhood when anyone hinted that rather than a flaw, I was the possessor of some gift.

Once identified as having this gift, I felt liberated. The following year I began something of a meteoric blossoming in intellectual ability. I began, in short, to grow into myself.

During the seventh grade I entered the school science fair with an electric motor I had built. I settled for honorable mention rather than first place because I had simply not bothered to concern myself with learning a whit about the electromagnetic principles that caused the motor to run.

The motor was for me an intuitive design. That it corresponded to the laws of electromagnetism was fine with me. It had simply never occurred to me that I would need to know anything in advance in order to design and build the thing.

As a result, the judge's question to me, "How does it work, son?" caught me somewhat off-guard.

Seventh grade was the year for honorable mention. Eighth grade was the year I hoarded all the honor awards at the graduation ceremony.

From the stage that night the principal announced those individuals who had successfully completed the test allowing them the privilege of attending Lane Technical High School.

I was prominent on that list.

Forest and I celebrated by talking deep into the night about our favorite books. We were on the way!

I should have known that for every joy granted in Cabrini, ten are denied. The cruel realities of Cabrini never took second fiddle in any orchestra.

Not a week after our graduation, a hideous wailing cry echoed in the underpass that ran along the first floor apartments at Cabrini-Green. It brought hundreds of faces to window screens and many older kids and adults out the door.

"No!"

I recognized that voice. It was Forest's.

His ten-year-old brother had ventured to the south side of Chicago to visit their older sister. He could never have known that destiny would cause him to intersect with a young boy who required only a victim in order to be granted entrance into a gang—the Blackstone Rangers.

He won his membership by severing the spine of Forest's brother with a single shotgun blast. The wild, animal screams of Forest's mother echoed throughout the night, keeping me—and I suppose many others—awake.

Forest started Lane Tech with me that fall, but I could tell that it was not knowledge that was filling his head. I knew it was the echo of a shotgun blast and the hysterical wailing of his mother.

Forest, my best friend, didn't finish Lane Tech. That shotgun blast took out more than a ten-year-old boy. It took out the heart and soul of a young man who held more promise than any other person I had known at Cabrini-Green.

I orchestrated a retreat of my own. I lived within the pages of HG Wells, Asimov, Thurber, Poe, Baldwin, London, Angelou, Parks, Emerson, Thoreau, O. Henry, Hughes, Clarke, Dunbar, Hemingway, Einstein, Steinbeck, Wright, Orwell, DeFoe, Williams, Hershey, Shakespeare and Bradbury. I sought refuge in the brilliance of their thoughts, prose and poetry.

I too thought, and I dreamed. If you could have looked within my soul then, you would not have been able to tell me apart from any other striving, desiring young man.

Only the noises outside my bedroom window would draw you back out from my soul; they would remind you that, not only was this "not Kansas anymore," this was someplace far, far worse.

Chapter Five

There's got to be a better way."

I remember my mother speaking these words to James when he told her he was signing up.

"It ain't your war," she told him.

He shrugged. "That's true," he allowed. "But they don't train me to fight the war that is mine."

My mother looked at her oldest son and, for a moment, she was stunned by the wisdom of his words. Still, she was determined to try and talk him out of his decision to join up. She knew only too well the draw of the service for young, black men in the ghetto.

"What do you think you'll get out of it?" she asked him angrily. "Didn't do nothing for your father, did it?"

James glanced down at the floor and shook his head. "No. I don't think it did."

"Then why d' you want to do the same stupid thing?" she demanded.

He was silent for a few moments and then, in a voice that was firm in its finality, he said, "I got to do something. I've had my high school diploma now for a year. It hasn't helped me much.

"Besides, you know what my lottery number was. If I don't go to them, they'll come looking for me. It's that simple."

She took some temporary solace in the fact that he signed up for the Air Force and was assigned to the base in South Dakota.

"How bad can it be in South Dakota?" she asked one day, to none of us in particular.

She got her answer when James came home and announced that he had volunteered for a tour of duty in Vietnam.

"I cannot bear that crap in South Dakota," he said simply.

It is hard to remember America during those years, during the late sixties. The campus protests. The surging flames of the cities. The assassinations. And all the while the backdrop of Vietnam.

Cabrini did not escape the anguish of the times. Far from it. It plunged deeper into anguish than it had prior to those years. The seething anger that followed the assassination of Martin Luther King swelled and shrank in fits of violence that came like birth pangs to Cabrini. Birth pangs that produced only a stillborn.

Cars foolish or stupid enough to venture on the streets that passed our projects were subject to bombardment by bricks, bottles and worse. The screeching of brakes, the breaking of glass, the squeal of acceleration—these became the soundtrack for those years, a soundtrack of anger and violence which was for me interrupted only by the voice of my own mother, bringing her melody forth in counterpoint to the ugliness of the times.

My mother still sang. She still hummed. But hers was only a small voice against the larger chorus of pain and hatred.

However, there were events singular in their violence and cruelty which pierced the full wall of violence which surrounded Cabrini as completely as Phil Spector's wall of sound.

It was summer. Of course it was summer, an extension of the long hot summers that lasted for years. It was July and two cops—a seasoned veteran and his rookie partner—walked their beat in Cabrini, making their way beneath the sweltering shadows of the projects.

Only a handful of cops were assigned such dangerous duty. To garner the "honor" of working a beat like Cabrini, a cop had to either believe fully in his own immortality or show in some way that he did not carry the hatred of the unfortunate in his heart—like many of his brothers did.

The red projects of Cabrini gathered around a huge field. I say "field" because no one really knew for what purpose it was intended when Cabrini's creators poured the block-high, concrete skeletons of the buildings clustered there. Only remnants of intentions remained. There was a bench; a single basketball pole without a backboard; a twisted patch of wire mesh that might once have guarded home plate; and dried and brittle stretches of grass, dusted by dirt and gravel.

Whatever its original intention in the minds of the architects and engineers of Cabrini, this field stood as an open wound in the heart of the Cabrini projects. A wide-open place of vulnerability, where there was no protection, no shelter.

On that day in July, whatever innocence remained in Cabrini was ambushed and murdered.

Death had never been a stranger to the projects; but this, this was different. The victims were not children of Cabrini. This time, it was The Man.

Whether they died in a barrage of gunfire, or by two single gunshots no one knows. All that was consistent in the telling were the subsequent screams of bystanders as they ran from the scene.

Left behind in the middle of the field were the crumpled and lifeless bodies of the two police officers.

America was at war in the rice paddies of Southeast Asia, but it was not until that July day that war was declared on Cabrini-Green. Unofficially, the Chicago Police Department and Cabrini-Green were at war. Caravans of police cars streamed through the projects for days upon days, halting on a moment's notice to exchange gunfire with unseen gunmen encamped on the walkways high above the street.

As is the case with most victims, Cabrini-Green only came to know the two murdered officers after they were dead. Television newscasts introduced us to a rookie cop who was young, too young to have had the time needed to become like many of his cruel and vicious mentors.

He was not just "The Man," but a young guy—little more than a kid—who loved children.

We didn't know that he often walked through Cabrini on his daily patrols and handed out candy to the children.

I remember how I felt after those newscasts. I remember nights, standing at my bedroom window and looking out at the dimly lit ramps of Cabrini, hearing the faint cracks of gunshot in the distance. I knew in my gut the terrible feeling that rookie cop must have had in the middle of that field—no place to run and no place to hide, praying for mercy from those who had never learned to be merciful because *no one had ever shown them what mercy was.*

There were ways out from Cabrini-Green. The rookie cop had one find him. James went looking for another.

My way out can be traced from the second floor window where I watched years of passing cars disappear down the two-lane street that disappears to the east of Cabrini-Green. Like all the other streets and avenues around the perimeter of Cabrini- Green, it was curiously and awkwardly angled so that it shied away from the projects.

At night the streetlights were overwhelmed by the blinking of the huge white and red "White Way" sign that jutted from the side of the White Way Sign Company's building.

Clybourn Avenue.

Like Goethe, Schiller, Larrabee, Berlin, and Dayton, Clybourn began, ended, and was reborn miles away from Cabrini. Their paths were curious entanglements. Tumbleweed roads. For a long time I stared out at those concrete strips and I could not imagine what the city planners had been thinking. Then I figured it out. The reason for the nonsensical run of those streets was simple—the determination to deny that Cabrini-Green rose in the middle of their path.

Clybourn Avenue plots a straight path out of Cabrini and towards Lane Tech. A direct run to dreams.

Saving Grace on a Less Traveled Road

In some distant past, those streets were most likely straight or pleasingly curved, lined with neatly trimmed lawns and gingerbread-styled single family homes with oversized picture windows.

There were probably bicycles left out on the lawns, wagons in the driveways, and fathers arriving home, honking their horns until someone came running out of the house to clear the path.

In my mind I could almost hear the children crying out, "Daddy! Daddy!" in greeting. Just like television families.

Whatever magic Clybourn Avenue held in the past, it was the only one of those tangled and tortured streets to hold any magic in the present for me. It was the way out.

Clybourn appeared out of nowhere just south of our building, where it broke away from Division Street, and plotted a straight path north. For that mighty stretch of Clybourn there were no curves, no deviations, no ploys or head fakes —only a direct run toward my own personal place of dreams.

Five miles of straightforward, no nonsense desire. Its starting point was in front of the green and white sign proclaiming the identity of Cabrini-Green's red projects; its ending point—its fulfillment—came at the intersection of Belmont and Western, a short block away from Lane Technical High School.

In spite of the tortured and anguished years of my youth. In spite of the small joys and large sorrows. In spite of the ever-heavier weight of poverty and despair, my way out was straight and narrow.

Like a clear note in one of my mother's hymns, the road that would carry me away from my inheritance of poverty and deprivation was laid out clean and perfect.

My intellect was prepared for Lane. My experience was not. I was breathless the first time I gazed upon Lane, rising up majestically in the midst of a vast sea of manicured grass. A tower stood straight and proud from its facade, displaying a colossal clock on each of its sides, as if to provide silent and sure testimony to the fact that within these walls Chicago's brightest labored each and every second of the day.

Within the walls of Lane a bustling city existed. A population of five thousand people—administrators, teachers and students—was focused on the task of academic achievement.

Each and every year, thousands and thousands of Chicago's junior high school students were tested as they competed for the few available freshman slots at Lane. Only the top one- or two-percent made it.

Those few joined Chicago's longest and best academic tradition. In September of 1965, Paul, Ken, Henry, Forest and I took our place in that tradition.

Unlike the other freshman students, our intellectual ability and potential was tempered by the wonderment of our new surroundings. I would later learn that sociologists and developmental psychologists had a name for it—cognitive dissonance.

The five of us carried that dissonance as surely as we carried pen and pencil. Our kinship and our bond relied on shared past experiences, which rendered our time at Lane a glittering jewel, one that we feared would turn out to be nothing more than an illusion that would vanish in the mist.

Lane was a brilliant diamond, but our beginnings forced us to fear that it was nothing more than zircon.

We were bound by our beginnings. In a whisper like a curse, like a prayer, in fear and acknowledgement we all named Cabrini-Green as

Lane Tech's tower stands vigilant.

our home and it was to Cabrini-Green that we returned each and every day, leaving behind the trophy-lined halls of Lane and its hills of manicured lawn.

Beginnings speak to endings. That is the way it is with people. A child raised in upper-middle class surroundings, with parents who are both professionals with advanced academic degrees; a child who has his own room filled with books, toys and computers, who eats three full meals on clean plates every day; this child will likely presume that he will go to college. That he will be a professional. That he will live in the kind of home he has been raised in.

So too the child of Cabrini. Raised in poverty, fed the indignities of life, sharing a room with three, four, or five siblings. Shivering beneath cold blankets in the winter because the heat has been turned off. Eating meager meals. Eating them fast because, yes, someone *might* just take the food from your plate. Seeing the gradual and complete process by which a father becomes less than he is.

The mark of Cabrini is as apparent as the mark of Cain. Our task, those of us who traveled that straight road north to Lane, was to somehow mask that ugly mark. To erase it was impossible. To want to erase it spoke too painfully against the people we loved and who struggled along with us and for us. To mask it, to somehow make the scarring go away, even if the underlying wound must remain, that was our task.

To lift ourselves up by the bootstraps we did not possess.

They said we were brilliant, the five of us. Objectively brilliant. But it was our very brilliance which rendered us suspect—to our families and to ourselves.

Henry sequestered his brilliance in a cloak of silence, making sure to display only enough of his intellect to keep the curious from examining him like a lab specimen. His strategy and his pose worked magnificently for him through grammar school. He breezed through, unnoticed and unscathed.

However, at Lane the teachers were a match for their brilliant students. They knew why Henry was there. At Lane, he could not hide and his internal chess game with his ability was called to task.

Poor performance was not tolerated, not even for the sake of his soul.

"Henry," I told him one day on the bus ride home, "you've got to turn in the homework assignment in English or you're going to fail the course."

He shrugged his shoulders. We didn't know enough then to understand that his fear of failure was the surest invitation to it. To make the attempt to succeed was to invite the very failure that we were all certain awaited us anyway.

Why make the effort then? Better to succumb without the attempt. That way, you had never really failed. Not really.

I did not have a name for this convoluted litany of underachievement and defeat, but I knew a place where it was worshipped—on North Avenue beneath the tracks of the elevated train.

There, defeat was a badge of honor and the ultimate defense against failure.

We were the children that society determined were beyond help. We sucked in that message, drinking in it with the breast milk which nourished us in our earliest moments of life. Defeat was the best we could hope for. To invest too much in the attempt, to dare to hope and dream—that invited failure, real failure.

Beneath the L-track on North Avenue; my father's place of refuge .

Saving Grace on a Less Traveled Road

Henry could not lift himself up high enough to dream and to hope that there was something attainable beyond Cabrini. His road out of Cabrini was Clybourn Avenue. His road back in was shorter, quicker and more slippery.

One day he stumbled into our ninth grade English class with tinted glasses balanced on his nose, tinted glasses that barely shielded his glazed, bloodshot eyes.

He hunkered down into his seat and he bowed and lurched through the class, somehow managing to remain in his seat until we were dismissed.

I never saw him again.

He had joined the congregation of lost souls. With his loss came the painful realization that the place of worship for that congregation was not beneath the el, but within the bounds of an ever-shrinking soul. That realization made me hurt for Henry. It made me hurt for my father more.

And it made me fear for myself in a way I never had before.

Ken never pretended he was anything than he was—a determined, hardworker. It was a lesson forced upon him by the need to survive Cabrini. He worked at everything he did, from softball to calculus. There was no middle ground for him. No slacking. Later his minor greatness did erupt. He ended up at the City College after graduation, where he made campus history by shutting down the school while leading a student boycott.

For Henry, Cabrini became the open, opiated arms of defeat and indignity. For Ken, Cabrini was the stimulus to work hard and harder, the threat of what awaited him if he relented for even a moment.

Forest could not escape Cabrini. The shotgun blast that severed his little brother's spine was his constant companion. The explosion of it filled his head, drowning out the lectures of our teachers and the admonishments of his friends.

We begged him to try. He heard his mother's hysterical screams. We offered to study with him. He saw his brother's bloodied body. We promised him our friendship. He felt only the emptiness of his sorrow.

His family moved out of Cabrini. His name disappeared from our class roster after our freshman year. With its disappearance, I lost my best friend.

The walls seemed to be closing in on me. However, if they were closing in on me, I could only imagine how it was for Paul. Among us, Paul was even more of an outcast. In the social stratum of Cabrini, he occupied the very bottom. A Native American, Paul did not even have the badge of color to guard him in the cruel corridors of Cabrini.

In Paul, I met my first real survivor. He displayed a versatility that allowed him to survive not only Cabrini but also a society that denied his very existence. Although society—in both subtle and blatant ways—frequently expressed its attitude toward us, it acknowledged our existence. It failed to do even that for Paul.

Paul did not even have the benefit of a powerful physique. On the open plains, before the white man came to America, he would have suffered as well. He was scrawny and wore thick- rimmed glasses.

Long before society gave him a name, he was a nerd.

He was, ultimately, a boy without an identity in the world. Until he came to Lane. At Lane, for the first time in his twelve years, Paul had to be reckoned with.

His scores on the entrance exam were so high that our teacher whispered the results in awe when she read them aloud. Our heads turned and stared at the boy in our midst, the boy who had been only a ghostly presence but who was now more real than he could imagine.

In my heart, I felt a giddy pride for him. I heard the teacher whisper his numbers and they were imprinted in my mind as a prayer. In those numbers I realized that there was hope, real hope.

No matter what happened, no matter what we were and no matter what we'd been, they couldn't ignore us. They couldn't pretend we didn't exist.

Paul gave me this realization. And for that, I will always be grateful. His name also disappeared from my class roster by the time we were ready to leave Lane. But I will always remember Paul — the scrawny, nerdish survivor who had reduced his teacher to a prayerful whisper by his brilliance. Plain and simple. By the flame that burned within his brain, igniting his soul.

For me, things remained the same. After James enlisted in the Air Force, he wandered in and out of the apartment while waiting to be shipped to his assigned base. Our escapades as younger children seemed to have receded far into the past. When I looked at James, I no longer saw a boy, an older brother. I saw a man, confident in uniform, certain and determined.

I did not take into account that the uniform was only cloth that draped the body of a boy from Cabrini.

One evening, he staggered in the door.

"James?" I asked, raising my head from the book I was reading.

There was no reply, only the unsteady beat of footsteps on the stairs. The door to the bathroom slammed shut behind him and, though he tried to muffle it, the sound of his retching.

I looked across the room and, for a brief moment, caught my mother's eye. The combination of anger, grief, disappointment and pain that registered in my mother's eyes was startling.

She, much better than I, knew the scent of alcohol. She had lived with that scent for twenty years. It permeated every aspect of her being and her relationship with my father. For her, it was the incense of defeat, ignoble defeat.

She knew my father only as a man and, try as she might to change him, she had to come to terms with his manner of defeat. But James, James she had brought forth from her womb. She had suckled him. Held him. Disciplined him and cried for him. She had fretted over the world into which he had been born.

She had, in short, been his mother. She was not about to allow alcohol to empty him out from the inside as it had done to her husband, my father.

I watched her as she tensed. Her hands gripped the armrests before, like a coil responding to the tension, she sprang from the chair. She rushed across the room and bounded up the stairs. With each step, she cried out the same question, "Why!? Why!? Why!?"

I heard her crumple against the locked bathroom door. I heard the quality of her question change as the minutes passed. From the angry, demanding "Why?" that had carried her from her chair and up the stairs, to a weeping, plaintive "Why?"

"Come on, Mama," I said, reaching for her.

She shook her head. "No," she whispered, refusing to move from the bathroom door, as if she feared that by doing so she would be abandoning James.

"It'll be all right," I said, trying to sound convincing.

I managed to ease my weeping mother up and away from the bathroom door. She leaned against me as I helped her back down the stairs, and for the first time, I realized that I was strong. I realized that, like James, I was no longer a boy.

I thought of James and all his resourcefulness. I considered his anger and realized that his anger moved him more than any other aspect of his being. I knew that if James' anger broke or dissipated then he would be left defenseless in the world that Cabrini taught him to know.

I returned to my book but I found I could not read. I was staring at the page but not seeing the words. I don't know how many minutes passed, but I remember looking up as I first heard the slow, steady footsteps of my father making his way up the stairs.

In all the years of my growing up, my father rarely gave me or any of us a whipping. He didn't have to. There was an untaught, preordained, fearful respect for him by all his children.

I watched him as he began up those stairs and I imagined that his ascent was made all the more difficult by the realization that he had to tell his eldest son not to do what he had done. Not to become what he had become.

"James, come on out of there," he said softly. "Come on out, son. I need to speak with you."

I heard the sound of the door opening, then the sound of my father's hand against my brother's face. Once. Twice. Not an angry, violent slap, but a softer smack, more appropriate for a toddler than a grown man.

My father left the apartment after that. He came down the stairs and walked right out the door. He never said a word about the incident. Not then, not ever.

James never came home drunk again. But a few days later, he returned home in his Air Force fatigues and told us that he had volunteered to go to Vietnam.

My mother cried. My father just looked lost.

My mother, too, had decided that she had to find some way out of Cabrini. If not physically then spiritually and emotionally.

Her path was dignity.

Unknown to any of us, she had been hoarding nickels and dimes and quarters for nearly a year. Coin by coin. She used each one of those coins for bus fare.

We never asked where she went during the day. I never even knew she wasn't home most of the time. I was gone early and returned late.

One day, I returned home before her. She came home soon after wearing the white uniform she had to wear at Passavant Hospital, where she had gotten a job as a janitor.

She pirouetted in her uniform as though it were a glittering, sequined evening gown.

"Mama . . .?" I asked, unable to utter anything else.

She was filled with pride that day as she told us how she had used the coins for bus fare to the hospital where she cleaned the doctor's offices.

In this world, unless we are completely and utterly beaten, we search for those things which give meaning and value – the strength to endure. My mother's new job served as a reminder to all of us and to herself that she was worthy. And if she was worthy, then so were we.

It was her unbridled recognition of self-value, a recognition never taken away by the realities of Cabrini.

Her self-value invigorated her constantly and chronically crushed spirit.

As she pirouetted in her crisp white janitor's uniform I was given one of the few glimpses of the true substance of the energetic, joyful little woman I called my mama.

"A blessing," she said, referring to the effort she had been required to put forth.

Her enthusiasm for her work was not dampened even when our General Relief checks were discontinued when she notified the Public Welfare office about her job. Nor was it lessened by her ten children, empty kitchen cabinets and a jobless husband waiting for her each evening at home.

She had a job. She was working.

"And the offices," she would say, her voice taking on a faraway quality, as if she were describing something in a fairy tale, "they have furniture in those offices handmade from single pieces of wood. They have crystal vases. Paintings on the walls. You can't even imagine it."

But her descriptions begged us to try. She spoke reverently of the diplomas arranged so neatly on the walls.

She dusted these diplomas carefully and when she described them to me, she was sure to emphasize the names of the colleges and universities that they had attended.

"You can go there too, Rudy," she told me. "You can do it."

I knew the names of those colleges and universities, knew them because they were constantly spoken of by my classmates at Lane. The names my mother spoke of so caringly evoked my own deepest hopes.

She spoke as though the care she took in dusting their diplomas was a laudable duty, as though these doctors greeted her each day with genuine feeling, grateful for the job she did for them.

Over time, she came to feel a certain protective allegiance to these doctors and their families, families that she had come to know through framed photographs and carefully posed, smiling faces.

She talked about these doctors constantly, until they became as familiar to me as to her. However, she did not do this out of any elevated sense of subservience. No, the real reason for her enthusiasm for these men was the unspoken hope and dream that one of her own children would accomplish what the children in those family photographs took for granted as a reasonable goal in life.

Enthusiasm aside, her hard work and long hours were wearing her down. We didn't have any idea how much until, a few weeks after getting her job, my mother collapsed in the middle of our living room while sweeping the floor.

Her high-pressured blood had rushed forth into the vessels in her neck and roared up into her brain, where a tiny vessel had ruptured.

I watched, paralyzed with fear and helplessness, as she clung to the handle of the broom while she slid slowly down its length to the floor.

A few hours later, she lay curled in a fetal position on the starch-stiffened white sheets of a metal bed in the intensive care unit of Henrotin Hospital—the very same hospital that had taken my Uncle Larry a few years earlier and never sent him back again.

My mother survived that stroke. But her survival did not appease the anger that had blossomed within me.

This anger grew until it began to numb my senses. It was directed at her for her relentless striving. It was directed at life's unfairness, along with an even deeper and unjust anger at my father who had been mercilessly weakened by the very same forces.

I uttered an oath to him, terrible in its sincerity and cruelty. "If anything happens to my mother," I seethed in an angry whisper, "I will hold you responsible."

While some of my anger was directed at my father, that anger lasted only a brief moment. As certainly as I knew anything, I knew that there was no room left in my father's broken heart for the sorrow of having lost the love of any of his sons, even for a moment.

My anger very nearly overwhelmed me before it finally dissolved into its usual receptacle—my books. Soon after, I purchased a small wooden desk from a used furniture store on North Avenue and plopped it in a corner of my bedroom. There, amid the piles of books I stacked on it, the world around me disappeared and the unimaginable became my firm reality.

I managed to use those books as walls to protect me from the ugliness of the world beneath my nose. Those walls demarcated a sanctuary that kept me safe.

I was so safe that the few times that my sanctuary was violated were times I would never forget.

A few days after my mother came home from the hospital I was engrossed in HG Wells' *Time Machine* when a single gunshot outside my bedroom window reverberated between the buildings of Cabrini.

"Man, they shot that dude!" a voice from the ramps cried out.

When I looked out the window, I suddenly found myself looking into the surprised eyes of a teenager still standing only a few feet away from my second-floor bedroom window.

He stumbled toward the center of the small patch of grass that stood only a few feet from our apartment.

Then he bolted upright, as if he had decided to stop fooling around and demonstrate to every one watching that he was fine, that it had all been a joke.

I had almost sighed a sigh of relief when he toppled over backward. He rolled on the ground to his stomach and then, clutching his stomach, he inched his knees forward until he was able to stumble up to his feet again.

His hands clutched at his stomach. Even in the dim evening light, I could see the blood beginning to seep through his fingers. He twisted and turned and then stumbled and trotted beyond the view from my bedroom window.

Outside, the evening grew dark. My reading lamp shone against my face. With each passing second, my own reflection grew more distinct on the glass window.

Only moments before I had been looking out at a young boy, shot in the stomach, struggling for life. Now I was staring into my own eyes.

I tried to turn my attention back to *The Time Machine*, but for that evening at least, I had lost the protection of my sanctuary. I couldn't focus on the words on the page. I switched off the reading lamp, grateful that with its extinguished light so too was my reflection—and troubled, questioning eyes—extinguished.

Chapter Six

Hopelessness was endemic within the concrete walls of Cabrini. That hopelessness took on added dimension when President Kennedy was assassinated. With his death, a tiny seed of possibility was crushed.

With the single shot that rang out in Memphis, Cabrini erupted. Smoke, fire, the wail of sirens and the incessant echo of bullets rang off the brick walls of the towering buildings of Cabrini.

I struggled to shut out this reality, just as I had struggled to shut out the reality of a world emptied of hope, dreams, and men who had the courage to try and make changes. As always, my primary source of solace was my library, which by this time was modest but substantial. Along with my library, I had the halls of Lane Technical High School.

Lane had been such a safe haven for me that I didn't even realize that the world was encroaching even there. I realized just how much the day I almost got shot.

The ghettos were roiling following Martin Luther King Jr.'s death. Anger, violence and hopelessness was palpable. When the anger could not longer be contained in the ghettos and black communities, the young men and women, made wild by their emotions, did what every good commuter does — they hopped on the Chicago Transit Authority and took their anger elsewhere.

At Lane Tech, this anger first took the form of teenage posturing and minor skirmishes between groups and cliques. But even there, within the halls of that sacred place, it didn't take long for the fiery embers of emotions to fan into serious conflagrations. Within a few days, the small conflicts had transformed into masses of howling, wrathful mobs—one black, the other white.

Even so, I didn't realize how serious the situation had become until I stepped into one of the restrooms between classes and found Steve, a twelfth grader, standing on one of the toilets as he poked around on a window ledge up above.

"What the . . . ?" he stammered when I came in.

"Hey, Steve, what's up?" I asked, looking at him curiously.

Once he saw it was me, he struggled to regain the balance he'd had before my unexpected entrance. He managed to steady himself but, in the process, he swiped his hand along the ledge and knocked a black, snub-nose pistol off its resting place. It plunged into the toilet.

It was my turn to be surprised. "What the hell's going on, Steve?"

First, he sheepishly fished the gun out from the toilet and then rammed it into one of the tennis shoes draped over his shoulders. "Rudy," he said, never looking at me directly, "things are getting pretty hot around here. You know what's going to happen today after school, don't you?"

"Are you crazy?" I demanded. "What are you going to do with that thing?"

I couldn't believe it. I had lived on the same block with Steve on Sawyer Avenue just a couple of years before we moved to Cabrini-Green. He was one of the first black students to come to Lane.

In my old neighborhood, the magnitude of his brilliance was proverbial.

Now, only seven years later, I found myself facing him in the restroom of Lane Tech High, trying to convince him not to do anything that could ruin his life.

"Steve, you haven't even given yourself a chance yet. Don't blow it. Please, don't blow it."

"It's not up to me Rudy," he said in a voice that struggled to convince itself. "I gotta do the right thing here."

"The right thing? You think that doing the right thing has anything to do with that?" I demanded, looking at the sneaker hanging on his shoulder.

He shrugged. He tried to look me in the eyes but found himself looking away. "I gotta go."

As I watched him leave the bathroom, I realized that those forces that had somehow convinced him he had no choice were the very same forces that had driven so many others to solve life-threatening problems with life-threatening acts.

For the remainder of the day, everyone at school was on edge. Every time one of the fire alarms was set off, classes dutifully emptied out into the field behind the school. There, students glared at one another, silently prodding each other toward the very acts that we all feared.

We had spent so much of the day outside of the classroom that it was actually difficult to tell when school was finally dismissed for the day. Long before the final bell, groups of students had wandered off campus, positioning themselves on every street corner. Waiting.

The black students had gathered at the corner of Western and Addison, where they waited in mass for a bus. In spite of the tension, I decided to stick to my usual routine, to walk the distance down Western to Clybourn, where Ken and I usually caught the bus back to Cabrini.

I had no desire to become mixed up in the turmoil and battles of the other students. I had already become too familiar with death.

In a child, this familiarity has the tendency to numb the senses, turning real fear into little more than an annoying anxiety. I knew that anxiety as I started down Clybourn with my usual bundles of books under my arms.

I was halfway down the block when I first noticed the small entourage of white schoolmates keeping pace with me on the far side of the street. I looked up into their angry faces.

"What's the matter? Scared?" one of them yelled.

Several feet later, there was another taunt and then another. Dares to cross the street. Angry threats.

While I wasn't frightened, I was no fool. When the mob realized that I was not going to play into its hands, it stopped mid-block and granted me passage.

Suddenly, a block later, I was stopped by the sound of Ken screaming to me from half a block away.

"They're coming, Rudy! They're coming!"

I looked up to see him running toward me, his arms flailing as though he were trying to take flight. Behind him, his books and notebooks were strewn all over the street.

Further down the street, I saw the Western Avenue bus rapidly approaching the intersection. It was filled with black students, their arms and heads sticking out from every window. Beyond the bus, I could see hundreds of screaming, stone- throwing, bat-waving Whites.

The light turned green just before the mob caught up with the bus. It rolled through the intersection, right past me and then disappeared further down the street.

Just then, the crack of a gunshot pierced the air. The back window of the bus exploded.

"Rudy!" Ken cried out. "They're shooting!" He was still running, chasing after the bus.

Suddenly, a barrage of gunfire erupted from the mob behind him. I could see puffs of smoke rising above the mob each time a gun fired.

I was rooted to that corner. Bundles of books under my arms. Staring at death coming my way.

"I wonder what it is going to be like to be shot," I thought. I felt strangely calm. I wasn't frightened by the death that would surely follow.

Then I smiled to myself. I couldn't help it. The irony of the situation was just too rich. It seemed that I would not perish in Cabrini-Green after all. I had survived the projects. Of course, it seemed that I would perish at the hands of the very forces that had helped forge the substance of my origin.

I watched Ken sprint across the street and dash past me into the open door of the tavern that stood on the southwest corner of Clybourn. Just as he dove through the door, a bullet smashed into the doorframe.

Still I stood on the corner. Waiting for mine.

Instead, the gunman pointed his gun into the sky and sent a barrage of bullets into the air. At that very moment, the Clybourn bus pulled to the curb in front of me. The bus driver didn't wait to figure out what was going on.

That incident blended imperceptibly into the violent, singeing summers that followed. It was simply engulfed by the nightly news all over America—vision upon vision of cities perishing in conflagrations. I don't know what happened to Steve. I suppose we would have made the news also had he or someone else died. But long after the angry confrontations ended, that incident remained impressed on my memory. For me, it epitomized the emotional and physical price I was to pay for my journey out of Cabrini.

I saw it all clearly yet it did not hinder my growing determination to put as much distance between myself and 630 West Evergreen as possible.

In spite of the tension, Lane was still my road out. Lane's curriculum structure was very much like that of a college. Each student had to choose an area of specialization before graduation—science, drafting, math, English or music.

Science fascinated me but I was drawn to drafting by an absolute love of the lay of the lines upon the page. Unfortunately, that love was deadened by the relentless unfairness of my drafting teacher.

It did not matter how hard I tried to produce flawless work, he seemed compelled to give me an average grade. Each time I looked at my mark, I would come away troubled and confused. I could not understand. Once, I intentionally submitted faulty drawings just to test him. His response was the same.

Clearly, he was not examining my work at all. I could not tell if this was his way of remaining noncommittal or if it was his way of subverting all the high grades he was forced to look at on my report card each and every time he had to grade me for the class.

Math was never an option for specialization. I was, in a word, inept at the subject. Music came naturally to me, as did my profound joy in it.

By the time I reached my senior year at Lane, I had become a National Merit Semifinalist and had earned placement in the top five percent of my graduating class of nearly two thousand.

There followed a flood of letters from universities to our rusted, doorless mailbox in the breeze way at Cabrini. The letters and attention were flattering, but I could not decide what I should do.

"Rudy. Telephone," my mother called up to me one evening.

I rarely, if ever, received telephone calls.

"Yes, is this Rudolph Willis?" a male voiced asked.

"Yes it is," I answered.

He announced that he was calling from the office of one of the Senators from Illinois. "The Senator has chosen you as his selection to attend West Point," the man explained. "Would you like to attend?"

I probably would have given the offer more thought if I had gotten from his manner and tone that he was interested in anything other than getting off the phone as quickly as possible. He must have known he was calling Cabrini.

"I have not considered West Point, no sir," I told him.

"I'll inform the Senator."

That was the last I heard about West Point.

I suppose that I should have been giddy with the offer, as well as the other offers pouring in. The fact is, I was struggling with that cognitive dissonance again. I was in transition. What I had wanted for so long—getting out of Cabrini—was soon to be a reality. But before I could move forward, I was caught in a long look at where I was, at my family, the people I loved.

Life had, for a brief time, begun to be more fair to my father. The Seeburg Jukebox Company had hired him. Every day when he returned home from a day of work, there was a smile on his face. For the first time in his life, he had been given the opportunity to do something he liked. To work an honest day's work at something that called into play his intelligence and his ability.

More than that, he was proud of the fact that he was the first black person who had ever sat on Seeburg's electrical assembly line.

"I feel good about that," he told me one evening, in a quiet, dignified voice.

One Saturday, he went out and he bought a fifteen-year-old Chrysler Imperial. It was dull gray with shark fin fenders and a fake wheel on the trunk. When he came home, he ran his hand lovingly over those fins.

It was the first car he'd owned in twenty years.

"Yes, sir," he said. "I think we've finally turned a corner."

If Cabrini taught its inhabitants anything it was that there was no such thing as "turning a corner." A few months later, Seeburg closed down its assembly lines and went out of business.

In case he didn't quite get the picture, a few days later, my father went out to start his car and he found a thick, brown sugar bubbling out of the gas cap. Clearly, someone in our building had decided he had come too close to the fulfillment of a few of his meager dreams.

The car sat in front of the apartment for a few days until he was able to get a tow to the garage, where one of his buddies was going to try and fix it.

"Rudy," he said to me not too long after that, "take a walk with me to the garage, would you?"

I remember well the times I walked with my father, because it wasn't often that any of his children got a chance to spend private moments with him.

As we walked, I was conscious of how much longer my legs had grown. When I was a boy, I had to struggle to keep up with him, even though he moved at a nice, slow, easy gait. Now I felt as though I had to slow down for him.

We walked in silence for several blocks. "Well, Rudy," he said, breaking the silence with his considerate voice, "I guess you'll be done soon, won't you?"

I knew what my father really wanted to know. Although our way of life had long before destroyed his capacity to share directly his life with his children, his reserved presence hovered distantly, constantly. He was, in this sense, always close by in the evolving lives of his children.

Even as a child, I always sensed his reticent savoring of the bits and pieces of himself that he must surely have recognized in each one of us.

I was always drawn to the pages of books but I had another love as well, one that was a direct gift from my father—the love of music.

I had purchased a jet black, ivory-knobbed electric guitar from a pawn shop on Chicago Avenue. With a tiny record player as a guide and teacher, I submerged myself in the euphonious world of Motown, followed by a passionate command of Wes Montgomery and B.B. King.

There were times when only the soft, delicate sounds of my guitar reverberated among the buildings of Cabrini, heralding the first lights of dawn.

This had been during the mid-sixties. The Motown sixties. In ghettos all across the country, inner-city black kids were plucking on guitars, banging on drums and stepping up to makeshift microphones in their attempts to mimic the Hitsville sounds of Detroit.

Who didn't want to make the Jackson Five's destiny their own?

My brothers, Steve, Brian, Ronald and I were no exception. I purchased a three-piece drum set for Steve and Ron and added a bongo for Brian.

Hearing us play together had lifted my father's spirit to heights he must have known when the music was his own. He even offered to be our manager but, after a few days of sober attentiveness, he disappeared, returning a day later lost in the salvaging comfort of his alcohol.

We had walked another half-block before I answered. "I've been thinking about becoming a doctor, daddy." I glanced quickly at him. "But I'm not going to give up the music," I added, hoping he realized that I understood.

"Good, Rudy," he said, nodding his head. "Whatever you do, you'll make me proud. Always remember who you are—and how far you had to come."

I slowed my steps and looked at him. "You think you might make it to my graduation?" I asked him, struggling against my hopefulness.

He didn't answer. He had already slipped back into his private world.

When we got to the garage we learned that his friend had been unable to fix the car; it was towed back to the dealer, who still expected him to finish paying for it.

The night before my high school graduation my father left the apartment. "I'll be back soon as I can," he said softly.

He was supposed to return that evening with a suit for me to wear the next day for my graduation ceremonies. The hours passed into the following morning.

In the morning, I was wearing my white shirt and a pair of well-ironed jeans when he came through the door with an outlandish, lime green suit he had bought on Maxwell Street.

"Like it?" he asked.

Like it? I loved it. It was the best looking suit I'd ever seen. It was also the first suit I'd ever owned.

"I'll come along to the ceremony with your mother," he told me.

He never did make it. My mother came alone.

I saw even less of my father the summer following graduation. My mother told me he had gotten a job driving a cab. But my mind was preoccupied with the prospect of things hoped for.

Of all the offers I'd received, I decided to attend Northwestern University in Evanston. On the day I was to leave, my father showed up in his Yellow Cab and drove me to the campus.

"Got to be around here someplace," he said as we searched for the Lindgren House and my assigned dorm room.

When we found it, he insisted on lugging my rope-tied suitcase up the four flights of stairs himself. When we were in the room, he walked over to the window and gazed out.

"Kinda small in here, don't you think?" He turned and looked at me for a moment before turning his gaze back to the window. "Rudy, you going to be okay?"

"I'll be fine, Daddy."

Still looking out the window, he reached into his pocket and pulled out a handful of crumpled dollar bills.

"That's okay," I told him. "You don't need to give me anything." That summer I had gotten a job working as a janitor at Bell telephone. So, instead of taking the money my father offered, I took twenty dollars from my wallet and handed it to him.

"Rudy, you got more money there than your old man," he said as he neatly folded the two ten-dollar bills and placed them in his shirt pocket. "Thanks, Son."

"Don't worry, Daddy. I'm going to make it."

"Remember what I told you, Rudy, and you will." He patted me on the back and slowly descended the stairs.

Months later, I found out from my mother that my father repeatedly asked about me for several weeks. I never heard it from him though.

There was only one other time that I ever had a chance to give my father something. Seven years later, when I was a third-year medical student, I came to visit him in his hospital room. I gave him twenty dollars again, this time to have his television turned on and to buy a pack of cigarettes.

He died two weeks later.

Chapter Seven

Once at Northwestern, I struggled to shut out the realities of Cabrini-Green. I tried not to look back. My world consisted of biology, chemistry, physics and physical chemistry. It was a world understandable, challenging, demanding—a world in which I was a worthy participant.

During each weekend and each school break, I was forced to descend back into a world in which I was anything but worthy, in which I was little more than potential victim. Each break saw me board the L-train for the short ride south back into the inner rings of my own personal hell, back to the turmoil of the projects.

There, I not only held a front row ticket to one of the most devastating family dramas going, I was also a participant. My father's alcoholic binges had grown more damaging. My mother's violent reactions had become even more violent.

There was precious little music in our apartment during those days. There were, instead, arguments, empty kitchen cabinets, fear and trembling. Swarms of roaches moved through the apartment, fearful of neither the light nor the dark. They refused to let me indulge in the worlds hidden between the pages of the books piled high in my bedroom. And outside, gunshots reverberated between Cabrini's wire mesh ramps.

During those visits to Cabrini, I followed a ritual that I had begun while still at Lane Tech.

At Cabrini, stone stairwells ascend relentlessly a full sixteen flights above the streets of Chicago. I often climbed those stone stairs to the sixteenth floor. Only there, at the top, could I find any splendor and beauty. By blocking out the towering projects nearby—and the noises of the ghetto below—I could imagine standing upon one of the private

72

patios which jutted gracefully from one of the elegant gold coast sky-scrapers dotting the coast of Lake Michigan only a handful of miles away. To the east, the view was—and remains—awesome in its beauty. The slender outline of Lakeshore Drive embraces the sandy shore of Lake Michigan as it stretches along Chicago's eastern most limits.

I would trace the winding ribbon of Lakeshore Drive as it cut north-ward toward some other place hugging the rim of Lake Michigan's waters.

Evanston lies along the northern shore. When I discovered that this enclave of imagined serenity was the home of Northwestern University, I decided that it was there that I would spend my undergraduate years. The Arlington Leadership scholarship I earned after graduating from Lane opened the second door in my journey from Cabrini. Picturesque Lakeshore Drive defined the path.

Even during those weekends and school breaks when I returned home, I would climb to the top of Cabrini to gaze in the direction of Northwestern's buildings, sprinkled almost imperceptibly among the exquisite two-story brick and white-framed homes that occupy Sheridan Road, just north of Loyola University.

Sheridan begins where Lakeshore Drive ends, turning Lakeshore's sweeping six lanes into a bucolic two lane road that meanders ever north-ward as it passes through the heart of Northwestern's campus.

There is another path that passes through Northwestern, one not tolerant of traffic, of cars and trucks. This path weaves its way along Northwestern's lake front, untouched by the crowds of students tramp-ing up and down Sheridan along their most efficient route to and from class.

Efficiency of that sort was not my concern at Northwestern. I chose to slip past the Arts and Science Library, to stroll under the stony bridge of the Biological Sciences building and up a block-long hill to a se-cluded patch of land between the lake and the three-story, white, stone, cylindrical building that houses Northwestern's telescope.

A short distance further along the main path branches off again, sending out a narrow, cobbled path that leads directly to Lindgren House where, on the fourth floor, I occupied a tiny room.

In my four years at Northwestern, this was the only path I chose to walk. It mattered not where my classes were located on campus. I found some way to include this path wherever I had to go. It led to a small sanctuary on the lake, where I could sit and gaze across the gray expanse of water and find some place beyond time and space untouched by the troubled world that had bred me.

My sanctuary was always short-lived. The distance from Cabrini was both eternally long and infinitesimally short. I had left my home but it had not left me. Weekends at school found me sitting at my desk wondering how long my mother, my father, my sisters and brothers could continue to survive. During those times, I dreaded the ringing of the telephone, fearing that the voice on the other end would tell me that someone had finally succumbed.

Many times the wait and the fear were more than I could bear. At those times, I would stuff my dirty clothes into a small, vinyl suitcase and walk hurriedly to the L-train that would send me back, back through the rings of my hell, back to where I would emerge from the Clybourn subway tunnel, two short blocks from Cabrini.

There, I would remain barricaded in my cinder block room, desperate to soften the relentless harshness of the life my family endured by

The view from my second story room at Cabrini: A church stood across the street between us and 1160 Larrabee.

immersing myself in the hidden universes defined by the laws of physics, chemistry and molecular biology.

I sought to impose the rational order of those worlds on the world in which I existed.

I often failed.

It was a time of riots, sit-ins, political upheaval and the examination of the American conscience. My father continued his intoxicated vigils. My mother chanted and hummed her prayers every night, praying that my brother, James, would not return home from Vietnam in a body bag.

Weekends were glimpses back at hell. Summers were raging visits, and they were the most difficult times. They were spent in desperate search for a job to supplement my scholarship. For two summers I managed to get a job as a janitor at the phone company.

My only respite during my search for summer employment came in the biology lab of my science advisor, Dr. Welks. I washed glassware and prepared biological solutions. His lab became like a second home to me when I wasn't in the library or in class.

There, in a forest of petri dishes, graduated cylinders and flasks, my love of research first took root.

Dr. Welks was a source of constant support and encouragement. Without his help, I doubt that I could have stayed the course throughout my third year, when the emotional toll of my history was becoming overwhelming.

Sometime during my freshman year at Northwestern—I can not pinpoint exactly when—a deep melancholy descended upon me. In spite of the achievements of that year and the years that followed, it continued to weigh me down, stooping my shoulders, making me feel not only older but ancient, convincing me that I had seen the sadness in the world and had no reason to believe the world held anything but.

That melancholy, which enveloped me like a heavy fog, did not dissipate until three years later, when the bright hope of my future finally shone through even that darkness.

Even though I had spent the required years to earn my degree at Northwestern, my life-saving education did not come from the spacious lecture halls, or from the bowels of dusty libraries. It came from the enduring effects of briefly knowing three individuals.

Rabbi Vogel showed no surprise when I settled into my seat among the Jewish students on the first day of his course on the Old Testament. Instead, he hovered over his precious old text at the front of the class and filled me and the others with the endless wisdom found in Job and Ecclesiastes.

Dennis Brutus was a poet. Not just a poet, but a poet whose words had shred the sinewy hearts of those in South Africa who had destroyed his people endlessly. He had come too close to spending a lifetime behind the stone walls on Robben Island, so he had fled to America. During his course on South African literature, I once interpreted a poem by one of his compatriots. The praise from Brutus would echo in my mind for years. For him, it would be years before he could go home.

Doctor Welks' enthusiasm for all that he did was infectious. But more infectious was the unquestioned confidence he had in my ability. I cheered silently for him when he later became the head of the biology department. He became more than a teacher, employer and advisor. He became an inspiration.

With the help of this rabbi who taught me about the Old Testament, this black poet who had fled the unjust sentence imposed on him by South Africa, and this scientist whose guidance was not determined by inflated self-worth or prejudice, I went to an interview at Washington University Medical School during my junior year at Northwestern. There, I encountered men and women whose brilliance—and whose respect for my own abilities and potential—simply dazzled me.

"What aspect of biology did you find most challenging?"

"How do you think that physics might help you in your medical career?"

"If you could choose where you would like to practice medicine, where would it be?"

So many questions, each asked with careful forethought and with diligence to my considerate answer. I enjoyed the questions about my academic experiences completely. I struggled more with questions about where I saw myself after medical school.

Where would I practice medicine? I feared to give my answer because I could not quite balance my own desire to be the best doctor I could be—no matter where that led me—with an answer that I thought they might want to hear.

I couldn't really see beyond the next step. To be the best. To be a doctor. It was a danger to look too far ahead. A greater danger to look too far behind.

The distance between that interview and Cabrini-Green could not be measured in miles, in experience, or even in academic achievement. I had been graced with the ability — and the luck — to make a quantum leap, one which carried me light years from where my history destined me to go.

It was dizzying. Frightening. Confusing. It was electrifying.

I was accepted to a position in the Washington University Medical School class of 1973 during the first semester of my senior year at Northwestern.

I wanted never to look back.

However, the past does not allow us sanctuary for long. None of us can escape from who we were. Indeed, until we understand who we were we have scant chance of realizing who we are, or who we are capable of becoming.

The dichotomy of my existence—my history and my academic ability—continually tore at me. At times there was joy, joy unimaginable to me when I was growing up in Cabrini. There was also anguish of a sort that I had never known possible in that concrete jungle.

In that cauldron, the brew that would become me was being stirred.

Chapter Eight

A slender line of crimson—just a trickle of blood—trailed behind the unwavering, sure path of the thin blade of the scalpel as it swiftly passed down the front of the iodine-scrubbed stomach.

Beneath the green surgical drapes lay the rest of Mrs. Jones, of whose presence we were reminded only by the rhythmic gush of oxygen down the plastic tube entering her windpipe and the vigilant, mesmeric beep of the fluorescent green oscilloscope overhead that monitored her heart.

"You see, Rudy. Nothing to it." Whittico said from behind his surgical mask. "It's all in the hand, son."

The surgical incision, traced by Whittico's blade, looked like it had been painted there—nothing like the gaping wounds and spilled bowels at the other end of the knives wielded at Cabrini.

I had left Chicago only two weeks before to spend the summer before the start of medical school under his tutelage. It was to be a summer of christening by one of St. Louis' most prominent surgeons.

Whittico tossed the scalpel into a metal tray, flipped his hand over, palm held to the ceiling, and deftly grasped the new knife slapped into his palm by the surgical nurse at his side. This he did in a continuous movement, as though it were a part of a well rehearsed dance.

"Well Rudy, since this is your first case, you might as well start learning," he said, glancing over his shoulder in my direction.

I nearly toppled from the stool on which I stood behind him.

I hesitated, then whipped my hand, palm up, into the air.

The operating room immediately filled with snickers.

Doctor Whittico's amused eyes peeped at me over the rim of his surgical mask.

"I can see already, Rudy, that you're going to be a hell of a doctor," he said. "But I think Mrs. Jones would be pretty upset if she found out later that you had taken out this tumor and she had paid me for just standing around."

A round of snickers started again. The surgical resident's ended with an admirable, knowing wink.

Whittico's second incision splayed open Mrs. Jones' abdomen like the pages of a book, ready to tell us the story of her stomach problems.

Methodically, he would nab a bleeding blood vessel with a pair of elongated tweezers, and lift the vessel's end into the air for the few hand-flurrying moments it took the surgical resident to tie off the bleeder. Their movements complemented each other in an orchestrated display of timed precision and dexterity, a display that could compete with the best that ballet has to offer.

"If you look just beneath the tip of my scissors," Whittico explained, pointing to a swollen mass of gray tissue, "you can see the cancer buried in the head of the pancreas."

As though given a cue, the surgical resident pivoted on his heels, scooped two large metal retractors off the surgical tray, pirouetted, and then slipped their ends effortlessly into the crevices of the gaping incision.

Whittico held up a hand without looking up from the undulating waves of glistening pink bowel that filled the wound.

Swiftly, the nurse shoved another surgical glove over his gloved hand, without waiting for his request.

He gently plunged his hand into Mrs. Jones' abdomen and began to carefully probe, periodically hesitating while caressing an organ, as though his fingers were giving his mind's vision another snapshot of what lay inside.

"We got a sweep here," he said. "Looks like it's all still sitting in the head of the pancreas."

The resident loosened his grip on the retractors and spun around again on cue, shoving both hands into the air. The nurse snapped a second pair of gloves over each.

"Well, Rudy, its time to go to work," Whittico said.

What followed was only partially understandable, but magnificent.

Whittico's blade began to dissect, slice, tease and sever at a furious pace. Unpredictably, he would cease for a moment to point out an important part of the anatomy.

"This is the distal end of the stomach, it enters the duodenum . . ."

"The duodenum sweeps around the head of the pancreas." He pointed. "Here both the bile duct and pancreatic duct enters the duodenum . . ."

"Underneath here," he pushed aside a portion of the liver, "lies the gallbladder . . . "

Meanwhile, the surgical resident's hands moved in tandem—smoothly, skillfully—lassoing severed blood vessels and tying them shut within seconds of the first driblet of blood.

Two hours later Whittico lifted the cancer from Mrs. Jones' abdomen.

The scene that played before me seemed surreal. It was a long, long way, mentally, from Cabrini.

I remembered how it felt as though the weight of my history had been left behind me when I pulled away from the curb and accelerated into traffic. Chicago's burnished skyscrapers and Lake Michigan's shimmering waves had given way to a canvas of wheat fields and open country side. Highway 55 put miles between me and my past.

Route 55: a straight shot to a different world.

Saving Grace on a Less Traveled Road

The two south lanes of Highway 55 did not swerve, wind or climb. They were like an arrow aiming directly for the heart of St. Louis below.

Two hundred and fifty miles later, St. Louis did not overwhelm me so much as creep up on me. It did not loom, surface or soar from the plains. Rather, it simply sprawled into the path of Highway 55 where it merges with Highways 70 and 40 on the west side of the Mississippi.

Its sole announcement was the curving arch of the enormous Gateway Memorial rising on the Missouri side of the Mississippi.

A mere two hundred and fifty miles from Cabrini and I felt as if I had ventured into another country. Sparse. Quaint. Still.

But St. Louis' stillness vanished behind the swinging doors of the operating room, like it would vanish behind the walls of my medical school classroom, and the brown, stony facade of Barnes Hospital for the next four years. In these places, the world was different.

Without fanfare, Mrs. Jones, an oblivious witness to her own surgical salvation, was wheeled through the swinging double doors of the operating room and down the narrow corridor leading to the Intensive Care Unit.

"One down. More to go," Whittico pronounced, dashing through the doors, headed for the locker room. "Next stop, Homer G."

Homer G. Phillips Hospital was grand, but not in the luxurious sense. Its splendor was more of the august, imposing kind. The kind of nobility that is bestowed gradually as a result of being the sanctuary where generations of the poor fled with life-taking problems. If your bowels had been eviscerated by a knife, you went to Homer G; if a trucker hadn't bothered to stop for a light while you were in the middle of the crosswalk, you went to Homer G; if you had managed to fall off your two-story roof, you went to Homer G; if you didn't bother to take your high-blood-pressure medicine until you had a massive stroke, you went to Homer G; and if you ignored the stomach pain caused by your appendicitis for a week, you ended up at Homer G.

City hospitals don't have the luxury of being grand in the royal sense. Homer G was no exception. It had earned its authority by virtue of the streams of dispirited, downtrodden, battered souls that flowed through its doors every day.

81

Chicago had Cook County. St. Louis had Homer G.

We rocketed away from Fermin Hospital in Whittico's mammoth, gray Cadillac. After several wheel-screeching turns and ignored stop signs, he slid the Caddy up to the row of dull glass doors of Homer G, leaving it parked right in the middle of the street.

When he slipped his thin frame from behind the wheel, the patients gathered at the door stepped away from our path, as though granting the respectful distance allowed for royalty.

At first I thought this was strange. But then I realized that in him they saw the healer who dutifully came every week to attend to them— just as he did others elsewhere. A spattering of "Hey, Whittico" ushered us inside.

"When I first came to St. Louis," he said, slowing down his long, brisk strides just enough for me to catch up, "there was no Barnes Hospital. At least, not for us.

"Back in those days you trained where you could. Now, I can practice pretty much wherever I want. But I'll tell you, it's hospitals like this that will make you a great doctor."

By the end of the day, I knew exactly what he meant. One appendectomy, a cholecystectomy, mastectomy, colectomy, and various lacerations later, we were done. Twelve hours had come and gone since our marathon began. By the time I made my way back to the medical school dorm late into the night, I could do little more than plop into my bunk. The day had been overwhelming.

This is the way I would spend the summer before medical school officially began: predawn awakenings, scurrying sprints, and marathon sessions at the side of an awesome surgeon. Often my evenings were spent alone lying in my bunk, eyes fixed on the shawdowy ceiling above, marveling at the turn of events in my life. That summer—the summer of '73—was the beginning of the long and rock-strewn, nurturing path that would eventually take me to the halls of NIH and the lab of Doctor Robert Gallo. I was sure of one thing: my inestimable determination—a determination bred, nurtured and solidified by Cabrini-Green. My past, fueled by a fear of what it offered if I failed, had shoved me into the waiting arms of a future I felt had been stolen from someone else.

Other future classmates joined me that summer. They gathered from New York, and Baltimore and Atlanta. They came from Boston, Memphis, New Orleans, Durham and Chicago. Some of their names remain etched in my memory: James and Kweli and Dave, Stan, Calvin, Eddy and Nancy. Like me, they too came to get a head start in the profession to which we had chosen to give a significant part of our lives. In their midst, my solitude dissolved into friendships. My quiet evenings gave way to impromptu, rowdy parties and countless balmy St. Louis nights spent roller-skating to the sounds of Motown at Queeny Park.

Jim Brown started it all.

Jim had made his way to St. Louis by way of John Hopkins. And it didn't take the rest of us long to realize that Jim had every intention of continuing his young life—with or without the rigor of medical school.

I remember the day Jim arrived at Olin Hall, our medical school dormitory. He lumbered through the door, ducking his head down a few inches to clear its entrance. In each hand he gripped a huge suitcase, with two others pushed under his armpits. An enormous green duffel bag dangled from one shoulder. Jim was big.

We also soon realized that within that massive torso resided the soul of Peter Pan. Somewhere back in his life, Jim had decided that life's wellspring is an all-or-none deal. If you didn't draw its cupfuls of soothing sustenance daily, it could be too late before you found the end of your life surrounded by arid emptiness. Jim had no intention of allowing this to happen.

A few weeks after everyone's arrival, Jim's husky frame was blatantly absent from our usual evening gatherings. All kinds of rumors floated among us concerning his obvious deviant activities. One Saturday I caught him sneaking down the dormitory's back stairwell.

"Hey, Jim. What's up?" I inquired, searching his face for any telltale signs of mischief.

He glanced over my shoulder sheepishly, making sure no one else had seen him. "Just checking out for a few minutes. You know what I mean?"

Beside Jim's bulk, there was one other striking thing about him — his eyes. It was the way they tended to bob around that caught your attention. The birth defect had resulted in a continuous jerking of his eyes, giving the impression of feigned craftiness.

"I need to get away," he told me. "Head for the park or something."

"You kidding? We don't have time to do that. We're here to get ready for fall classes."

"Look Rudy," he argued, letting his eyes sweep the hallway again, "after our classes start in the fall, we'll be lucky if we see the outside world again for the next four years."

His jerking eyes stopped just long enough to emphasize his point.

For some, college is a time for social flowering. For me, it had been a time of burrowing deeper into myself. I had become something of a recluse during my years at Northwestern. My habits were borne of my many needs—academic, psychological and spiritual. The years of my childhood had simply taught me too well the depth of sorrow, danger and pain that awaited any participation in society. My sanctuary had become myself, but it was the only way my beginnings would allow me to begin extracting from life those promises that would be long — too long—in the exacting.

The words on my degree from Northwestern spoke one thing. The meaning another. The words spoke simply, stating that I had earned my bachelor's of arts degree, having fulfilled the requirements; the meaning was nearly overwhelming.

I had by my accomplishment proved that there was some justification, however slight, for the hope this society might hold out to all of its children. This was done despite the dashed dreams and lost goals of my family. There was this victory to cling to, to enjoy — with a full heart. I was going to medical school. That I would be the first doctor in the family had an almost absurd ring to it. Given my history, being first was implicit in rising above.

But I had not yet fully realized the price I had already began to pay. The possibility of creating the droughty existence for myself that people like Jim raged against.

"Come on Rudy." He urged. "Take a break man. It'll be okay."

Later, I found out what Jim had been up to. Skating. Roller-skating to be exact.

A muffled, rhythmic beat seemed to spread in all directions. It resonated among the summer-laden leaves of the trees and then drifted upward, hovering everywhere, just above the treetops. At the top of the hill where we stood it gathered around us, then tugged us downward toward a globe of fluorescent blue light emanating from a cluster of trees below. Forest Park pulsated to the sounds of Motown.

In the clearing, a swirling ring of gyrating skaters circled the perimeter of the gleaming rink in absolute unison.

Jim rented two pairs of roller-skates, tossed a pair to me, then disappeared into the whirling mass of bodies.

On that balmy Saturday evening, under a twirling star-filled sky, I skated joyfully back to my childhood.

During the rest of the summer I often went back to the skating rink. I even convinced Nancy and a few others of the need for this rejuvenating salve.

Then Jim started disappearing again to some other place, where, once again, he apparently had discovered another of life's wellsprings.

My jolting, whirlwind baptism into medicine continued. I rode shotgun in Whittico's Caddy as we careened up and down the streets of St. Louis, dashing among appendectomies, cholecystectomies, vagotomies, lacerations, gunshot wounds, mastectomies and colectomies. Seven weeks later, at the end of my apprenticeship, he arranged for me to spend a weekend in the emergency room at Homer G Phillips.

A singular event will forever fix the image of Homer G in my memory, an incident that still holds Homer G's undissolved reflection before me, always attempting to push aside the legion of remembrances crowded there. It readily paints in the shadowy edges of Homer G's sharp, jutting angles and towers, of perfectly aligned windows looking vigilantly upon the surrounding dilapidated bungalows, boarded storefronts and vacant lots. It actually seemed stately in the midst of its deprived surroundings, its intricately inlaid dusty brown bricks attesting to its lost grandeur. With this image always comes the memory of the heat.

The heat of St. Louis' summers seemed at times to be as merciless as its winter cold. There was something in the damp, hot air that steamed the blood of the unfortunate, the suffering and the losers; it seemed to awaken the suppressed frustration of long, jobless days and to fuel fires of desperation that often erupted into violence. It reminded me of Chicago.

When I walked into the emergency room, Jesse Benson, the resident on call, was sitting at the nurses' station with his feet propped high into the air on the back of a chair. He was engulfed by a cool air of confidence.

"Hey Willis," he said, dragging out the "s" while barely moving his lips. "Been waiting for you, man. When the sun goes down, we go to work."

The nurse pulled a wrinkled surgical gown from a shelf and slid it in my direction. "You better put that on," Benson said, "It can get kinda messy around here."

Benson was right. Moments later our first patient stumbled through the door, reeking of whisky and urine.

"Well, here comes Joe, " a nurse said. "He always shows up when he ain't got no place to go."

Joe staggered to the middle of the waiting area, suddenly halted, then tumbled to the floor and started convulsing.

Benson grabbed the alcoholic's beard, yanked his head back, then thrust a tongue blade between his teeth.

"Never give'm a chance to chump on their tongue, Willis," he told me, motioning for me to hold the tongue blade in place.

The nurse had already slid beside him, holding a syringe full of Valium and a bag of intravenous fluid.

By then the drizzling, renegade brain wave in Joe's head had burgeoned into a raging storm, showering every muscle in his body with a barrage of electricity.

He arched into the air like a bow about to break.

A disquieting thought drifted into my head. I couldn't help but wonder how many of the desolate old men and dispossessed old women heaped along the train tracks of Cabrini had succumbed for lack of a piece of wood placed between their teeth and a little attention.

Benson slid the end of a needle into a vein in the Joe's hand, then pushed in the Valium.

Moments later an opiated calm descended on our patient, leaving behind only a telltale twitch of the cheek one moment, the thumb the next.

"That's all there is to it, Willis," Benson said, sucking out two large syringes of blood through the needle.

"We just need to make sure there's nothing else floating around in his blood except one hundred proof. Then we punt him upstairs."

Several other patients had straggled into the waiting room while Benson was working on Joe. Already they had filled the benches and spilled into the few cubicles used for the more urgent problems.

Benson and I slowly made our way among them, stopping just long enough to peek in an ear, listen to a heart, or sew up a laceration. When we reached one of the cubicles, we found a disheveled young woman waiting inside.

She sat with her feet in the chair and her arms wrapped protectively around her knees. Her purse and its contents lay strewn on the floor beneath her. She had been raped.

"Hi," Benson said softly. His almost cocky demeanor had disappeared. "I'm sorry, but I'm going to have to examine you to see how badly you're hurt."

She lifted her chin from her knees, but her tear-rimmed, saddened eyes could hold their gaze on us for only a moment.

"Why did he have to do that to me?" she questioned in a broken whisper to no one in particular. She repeated it several times while the nurse positioned her in the stirrups.

Benson had to sew a six inch laceration down one of her thighs and tape wads of gauze over her shins, where the skin had been torn away when her attacker drug her along the sidewalk to a nearby alley.

I couldn't help but think of Bernitta, Yvonne, Andrea, Kimberly and Shinette—my own sisters. I watched those tears slide down the corners of her eyes to her ear lobes as she lay there, staring at the naked light bulb dangling overhead. The anger that rose in my chest was furious.

Suddenly, I realized that what I had chosen to do for a living was precious indeed. I would be given the responsibility for the care of human beings.

It seemed like forever before Benson finally stitched the last gash and bandaged the last bruise. All the while I wanted to somehow apologize to her for the ugliness of the world, as though the world's meanness was an acceptable excuse for what had happened to her. But then I realized that my apology was irrelevant. So I just stood nearby and listened to her soft sobs.

When Benson and I stepped back into the waiting room, only a few patients remained. One of the nurses was talking feverishly into the phone at the nurse's station. She held her hand over the mouthpiece and yelled at us from across the room.

"Doctor Benson, we got a hot one on the way!" Her ear went back to the phone briefly. "Little girl. Asthmatic. They have oxygen on her. She's in trouble."

Moments later the muffled, piercing scream of a distant siren drifted into the emergency room. Its pitch shifted an octave higher with each passing block.

Suddenly, the emergency room doors burst open, flooding the reception area with a kaleidoscopic burst of white, yellow and red light.

The ambulance attendants, still panting from their sprint up the ramp leading to the emergency room, lunged through the doors and frantically propelled the cot into one of the cubicles.

One shouted a clinical history to Benson, who was already positioned inside.

"She's six. Been wheezing for two days, mama says. They thought it was a cold."

On the cot sat a frail child with striking, large brown eyes—eyes that seemed to look right through you. She was desperately attempting to suck in the thin stream of oxygen that flowed into the oxygen mask strapped to her face. The muscles in her tiny neck tensed furiously with each of her breaths, before sending a strident hiss of air down her constricted airways.

Her large eyes magnified her look of desperation.

"Adrenaline, stat!" Benson shouted. "Give me an intravenous needle. We need a theophylline drip. Now!"

Benson quickly tied a rubber tourniquet around her wrist, smacked the back of her hand to make a large vein swell, then slid a tiny plastic catheter through the skin and into the vein.

"She's tachycardic, doctor Benson," a nurse said. "Her heart rate is one hundred and forty. Systolic blood pressure ninety and dropping."

"Let's get her on the monitor. And push a dose of terbutaline by skin."

One of the nurses swiftly attached several wires from the overhead monitor to the child's chest. The monitor blared on with a loud volley of rapid heartbeats and displayed rippling, fluorescent green waves across its screen.

"Give me a syringe and needle," Benson ordered. "She's beginning to look dusky. Damn! Her blood oxygen is way down."

Since she had been wheeled into the emergency room, her radiant, chocolate skin had turned to a dull ebony. Benson plunged the needle into one of her wrist.

A moment later he held up a syringe full of blood. It was purple. "Damn! She's acidotic. Get me a blood gas result on this. Stat!"

Abruptly her struggling breaths slowed down. A calm seemed to finally enshroud her exhausted body. This was reassuring, maybe the medicines were working, I thought.

Suddenly, the volleys of heartbeats on the monitor disappeared, leaving behind the blare of a straight line.

"We got an arrest here!" Benson shouted. "Get the paddles."

The nurse shoved me away from the table. Benson plopped the ends of the electrodes on the child's chest then pushed a button on the handle.

She bolted off the cot.

"Start cardiac massage," he ordered. "Give me a tracheal tube."

One of the nurses began to push methodically on the child's chest.

Benson pulled the child's chin back and aimed the long plastic tube at the back of her mouth. He slipped the tube deep into her throat and attached the end to a black bag, which he began to squeeze.

"Okay. Let's see what her heart's doing," he said.

The nurse stopped pumping. The monitor answered with the same shriek.

Outside the cubical, several family members had gathered. In their midst, I could hear the distinct sobs of the little girl's mother. It was the kind of weeping I had heard too often as a child.

He shocked the child several more times, stopping only to push another drug or to allow the monotone shriek of the cardiac monitor to fill the now silent room.

The mother's sobs transformed to a high-pitched wail, which seemed to flow into the room and merge with the monitor's shrill.

Benson picked up another syringe, but let it drop back onto the counter. Then he slowly walked out the cubicle to the child's mother. He looked weary.

The rest of the night we tended to the needs of the other patients, but no matter how serious these may have been, I simply could not get thoughts about that child out of my mind. Since childhood I had known death in all of its merciless guises, and I would surely contend with it again for the rest of my professional life. But this was different. In a moment, this comely child had passed through our lives, leaving behind an imprint of her existence that still tugs at my emotional past.

The events of the evening made me feel as though I had participated in a movie, now projected in slow motion over and over again before me. When I left the emergency room later that night, the mother was still weeping beside the child's cart, refusing to let the attendants remove her from her presence. And the young woman who had been raped sat alone, still waiting for the police to show up to get a report.

After the time spent in the emergency room, the sultry St. Louis air seemed fresh. On the way to the dorm, my thoughts wandered back to the weeks before, to the time I had spent at the roller-skating rink.

Jim had been right.

Chapter Nine

The fall of '73 came quickly, and the class of 1977 descended upon Washington University School of Medicine. We poured into Cori Hall—a small auditorium named after one of Washington University's Nobel Prize winners. Its wood-paneled walls and rows of straight-backed chairs reminded me of a movie theater, while still imparting a no-nonsense atmosphere.

After a few minutes of noisy stirring the class settled in, each choosing a seat, to which they would return religiously for the next two years — two years of endless lectures by a parade of thick-glassed professors. However grueling, the first two years of medical school amount to little more than an intense continuation of the attempt to grasp the facts and laws of the basic sciences. All to one end — becoming a doctor. Here we would learn organic chemistry, physiology, biochemistry, microbiology and immunology. Then histology, pathology, neurology and pathophysiology.

On the first day, someone dumped a catalogue-size stack of handouts into our laps. This was the beginning of a deluge of information that didn't stop for two years: "The Embden-Myerhof Glycolytic Pathway," "The Cori cycle," "The Glycogen Pathway," "The Red Blood Cell Cycle," "The White Blood Cell Cycle," "The Intrinsic Coagulation Pathway," "The Extrinsic Coagulation Pathway." There were so many pathways to go down and cycles to go around that we were lucky if we remembered how to get back to the dormitory each day after eight straight hours of mind-numbing lectures. I suppose that some of this had something to do with what I had seen in the emergency room that summer, but for some reason it was lost on me.

Like my classmates, I simply applied myself to the task. My evenings and weekends were consumed while I roamed around in the deviant enzyme pathway that resulted in Maple Syrup disease and tracked down the misanthropic culprit in the Coagulation Cascade that caused a hemophiliac to bleed to death if you didn't do something about it. Fast.

The driving force for these frantic years of mental overload was simple and absurd: not knowing what on earth the test for the course was going to be on. We spared no end to ensure that Washington University did not come to the conclusion that our class was a hoard of idiots. A week after the information barrage started, someone placed a small tape recorder at the feet of the podium. Within a few days, it had multiplied fifty-fold. There were recorders all over the place. Electrical cords ran in every direction, a mass of entanglement sending out wires to electrical outlets like a fifty-legged octopus.

One day one of the instructors glanced down at the morass at his feet and said, "I've been trying to publish this stuff for five years. I didn't know it had become so important."

The problem was that none of us seemed to know what was important, so we all shut down our lives for a couple of years to spend time with Cori's Cycle and The Sodium Pump of a cell's membrane, among other things. Although few of us believed it, we were told that what we learned those first two years would result in each of us becoming expert in the art of healing and easing human suffering. I still am not convinced. What I am convinced of is a lesson one instructor taught without the use of handouts, diagrams or intellectual meanderings.

"Ladies and gentlemen, good morning."

So began our physiology class, taught by Dr. Braden, a brilliant young neurophysiologist. With his introductory lecture, we all knew we were on our way to becoming some of the best-trained physicians in the country.

He brought to the task brilliance, depth of knowledge, enthusiasm. He had, at his young age, established a national reputation.

I considered myself fortunate to have been assigned to his laboratory sessions during the course.

I watched him closely.

Early in the semester, I presumed his thin frame to reflect its effort to contain an energetic, fiery intelligence. However, during the labs, when we were up close and huddled together over experiments at our lab benches, I could sense the brief throes of weariness. I noted the slight, momentary droop of his shoulders, the slowing of his normally brisk walk.

A hand, reaching out and clutching a bench top.

I looked into the eyes of my fellow students. Had they seen what I had seen? Inevitably, no. They had been oblivious to these small, fleeting signs as they clung to each and every tidbit of knowledge he shared.

"If you look, now, at the oscilloscope," he said, after giving a tiny electrical shock to the thigh muscle of the lab mouse restrained on the table, "you will see a spike in the sinusoidal wave. This is similar to what happens when a nerve signals a muscle to contract."

"You mean our brain shocks our muscles to make them work?" someone dared to ask, hoping the question wasn't too stupid.

"No. Not quite." Braden said. "Actually, there are chemical and electrical changes in the end of the nerve, near the muscle, that result in the release of a neurotransmitter like acetylcholine. This tells the muscle what to do."

Looks of enlightenment rippled through the group gathered at the bench.

"Now, I want someone to give it a try," he said.

A student poked the end of the probe against the mouse's thigh and pushed the button on the electrical transformer.

Suddenly, the mouse stiffened, started seizing, then lay deathly still.

There was a moment of uncomfortable silence as the reality of what had happened sank in. Then, one of the students said, almost cheerfully, "Looks like we just lost our first patient."

Nervous laughter followed and some small talk while we jotted down our findings.

Dr. Braden had been seated on a bench just a few feet away, alone. I knew he was there before I turned to look at him. When I did, I found him staring vacantly at the table which held the motionless, wide-eyed mouse we had been working on.

His gaze was vacant. Sad. Lost. For a moment I was profoundly troubled by it. Then, in an almost revelatory manner, I realized that the vacant look in his eyes was profoundly familiar to me. Indeed, it wasn't vacant at all. It was a gaze I had seen so many times as a child. Too many times.

It was a sadness so deep that it seemed to engulf everything around it. I did not know then the sadness which engulfed him, but from that moment on Dr. Braden had my complete sympathy and respect. Although we had each surely traveled different paths in this life, he had seen what I had seen and had come away with the same knowledge.

He too was one of the walking wounded.

Months later, during a neurology lab session, another instructor displayed a human brain to illustrate some of its anatomical characteristics.

"This patient had malignant melanoma, a deadly skin cancer," he said, almost in passing. "You can see the areas—here and here—where it has metastasized to the brain."

A wave of recognition brought me to attention. Doctor Braden had suffered from this same form of cancer, was suffering with it even as he taught our class months earlier, even as he accepted our thunderous applause at the conclusion of his final lecture.

And I knew, as certainly as I knew anything, whose brain had been on display that day during our lab session. The magnanimity of Dr. Braden's act was unforgettable. Even in death, he had claimed a small victory. He had found a way to continue to contribute to his passion and his profession—and to share his brilliance with those who had professed the desire to be as he was.

However, as I looked around the room, seeking some trace of recognition in the faces of my classmates, some sense of the significance of what was on display before them, I saw only a sea of expressionless stares.

I feared deeply that their hearts had already grown cold, an all too acceptable reality of our stern profession. That day changed the way I viewed both myself and my chosen profession.

The overwhelming amount of work in medical school provided a haven from my past. It protected me from both my past and my future. Time stood still for me then. It made time my friend.

But whenever the cares of medical school subsided, I was fully aware of what lay eastward, beyond the Mississippi. Chicago. Not the Chicago of song, of film, of theater. Not the mythologized Chicago.

No, the Chicago that beckoned me was a Chicago of tenements, of deprivation. It was the Chicago of my history. Of my family. Of my life.

Climbing to the roof of Olin Hall, I would look into the east as the sun set behind me. There, beyond the flat landscape of St. Louis, beyond the Mississippi, lay a place perfectly clear in my mind's eye.

There, the place of my father's own respite, somewhere along the Mississippi so long, long before. There, the place where my mother made music, and made music still.

In my mind's eye, I could still see the shimmering glow of the Windy City that had looked coldly upon my beginnings, the shimmering glow of the place where my father still abided and where all my sisters and brothers still managed to dream, the place where my mother continued to endure.

But my mother had not only endured, she had grown stronger, and her strength flowed westward to me through her many letters — letters which sustained me.

"Rudy, I too have toiled during stormy rains. But we must remember that the sacrifice we make is a minor price we pay to accomplish the possible. If I had ten thousand tongues, I couldn't say in words how much I love you as a son. You have been a loving son. God has given you what you need in this life and He has answered my prayers. For this I thank Him."

I took her strength and bolstered my own.

Life was no easier for her. After her first stroke, she had gone back to the business of guardianship of the family. But my father's health was beginning to fail, the last victim of his life of unfulfillment and drink. And although James had returned from Vietnam, he was not the same. His days were spent in a cloud of confusion as he roved from city to city, searching for a peace that had eluded him as a child and which never existed in the place he had gone to war.

There is a photograph of my brother after returning from that war. It is in the book, *Brothers*. In that picture his eyes seem to be searching as he stares into the distance, frozen forever in the photograph of him hidden between its pages.

I felt the loss of my brother as deeply as if he had been killed in the war. I cried, thinking back on those times we'd had together. Me and

A photograph from the book Brothers; *James is in the background, looking into the distance.*

my brother. The insanity of it. The shame of it. The closeness of it.

There was now one other problem my mother had to contend with: Bernitta. Bernitta was the eldest of my sisters and she was a joy to be around. As I grew older I began to realize why. She was born fourteen months after me, becoming both my big and little sister at the sound of her birth cry. The innocent simplicity that veiled her perception of life's events was admirable. But, it also enshrouded the little girl who never quite became a young woman.

Often I heard my mother lovingly speak about Bernitta's "slowness". The developmental milestones just never appeared when they should have as the years of my sister's life came and went, years that failed to give her even a brief understanding of the troubled world around her. Maybe this was life's way of appeasing the hardship of one of my mother's children, life's way of saying it could not redeem her from the pain, but it could lessen the sting by depriving her of comprehending its horror. As a result, Bernitta spent most of her school years in special education classes, where they tried to fix the unfixable.

One day she disappeared from the apartment. She was gone for days. My mother later found out that she had simply decided to go home with one of her schoolmates. His mother apparently finally decided to call my mother days later to tell her that Bernitta was okay.

Nine months later my sister had her first child.

Life had decided to protect my new nephew as well. You could easily see this in the vacant, listless eyes that peered at you from beneath his abnormally enlarged brow.

After my nephew was born, my mother immediately brought him into the loving folds of her arms, as she had done with her children and my cousins before him. She spent months battling the Illinois Department of Children Services in an attempt to become her grandson's permanent guardian—months that turned into years. The problem was only heightened by Bernitta's restlessness. She disappeared again from the apartment, this time with my nephew. It took months for my mother to find her. Bernitta had moved into a squalid, dank apartment in Uptown with her mentally retarded mate.

One day the police called. My nephew was dead.

He had been found crumpled on the damp wooden floor of the apartment. It didn't take long for everyone to realize the obvious. My sister could take care of a child little more than she could take care of herself. My nephew's autopsy report painted a picture of malnourished muscles, bedsores and pneumonia-filled lungs—lungs he couldn't breath with, lungs that tired and simply stopped working.

They took my sister away.

She has spent the past twenty years of her life in a mental health facility among the quiet streets of a bucolic Chicago suburb, a place where we could never have even imagined living while growing up in Cabrini-Green.

During those times, I felt crushed in the fulcrum of my past, present and future. I walked through the halls of the medical school and I felt as though I was peering through a kaleidoscope. White coats, stethoscopes and hallowed halls. Urine-soaked hallways. Broken elevators. Squalid Cabrini. Patients. Bernitta. James' eyes.

Chapter Ten

When the first academic year came to a close, I decided to remain in St. Louis and do an elective clinical rotation in radiation oncology rather than face another summer in Cabrini. My mother's return letter never questioned why. She seemed to know better than I the constant, unrelenting destructiveness of Cabrini.

I had been fascinated with biochemistry, genetics, physical chemistry and molecular biology during my undergraduate years. Then, my knowledge was rooted in the realms of the laboratory and the theoretical. On paper the many theories offered to explain cancer, one of the most challenging and perplexing diseases that plague us, were logical and compelling. In real life, the theories too often fell short.

During my clerkship, I was forced to look into the eyes of people, my patients, who suffered and who often courageously tried to live even while they were dying. In their eyes, I saw a reflection of the pain and suffering that grips deeper than the physical. In their eyes, I saw the veils covering the rent soul. In their eyes, I saw my future.

But, like my classmates, I had to start first with the basics. In medical school this means knowing how to examine a patient. After aeons of lectures, second year medical students would kill just to get a chance to slip into a white lab coat and play doctor. It's the only act that makes sense after spending endless years bound to lecture hall chairs, huddled over lab experiments, or incarcerated in the bowels of some dusty library. Washington University traditionally baptized its medical students into the real world of medicine by letting them run rampant up and down the corridors of Barnes Hospital during its introductory course to Clinical Examination.

Saving Grace on a Less Traveled Road

That first morning Cori Hall, once again, filled with the class of '77. But in place of the usual blue jean and T-shirt clad, bleary eyed congregation, gathered a throng of clean cut and prissy medical students. The change was so remarkable that it took a few moments for some of us to recognize each other. The change in attire varied from the simple to the outlandish. An added bow tie here, a short lab jacket there, and a hoard of full-length, starchy white lab coats everywhere else. One guy actually had on a three piece pinstripe suit beneath a spotless, crisp lab coat with his name embroidered across the lapel in huge red letters and a Hewlett-Packard stethoscope flung conspicuously around his neck as a way of telling everybody what he was or would shortly become. Clearly some of us had been waiting too long to get to this day.

After the usual pep talk from the Dean of Students about how we were about to enter an important and new phase of our training, we were paired off and given the names and room numbers of the unfortunate, afflicted souls waiting in the hospital for us to descend upon them. Stuart Levin and I were assigned the same patient.

You couldn't help but like Stu. He had been transplanted from New York, and he brought with him a subtle, brilliant Jewish humor that made you smile even when you felt like crying—no matter how bad things seemed to be going. But I had quickly realized that his easygoing demeanor was really a reflection of an admirable, unshakable confidence handed down for generations—that, and his intense intelligence.

Cori Hall emptied like a stampede of cattle.

"Now look Rudy, this is going to be a piece of cake," Stu said, shifting a huge black doctor's bag from hand to hand as we scuttled across Euclid Avenue to Barnes. "All we got to do is ask every question in the clinical systems review, even if the guy hasn't complained of a problem."

"Come on Stu, that'll take all day," I said, already skeptical of the approach.

"I'm telling you. That's the way it's done," he said, shifting the bag again. "Besides, I already checked with a couple of people in the fourth-year class. They should know what they're doing by now."

"Yea, they *should*," I said sarcastically. Stu chuckled.

We wandered around the halls for nearly thirty minutes before we finally found our patient's room, hidden at the end of the hall on the upper level of Queeny Tower.

Stu stood panting at the door, having lugged his doctor's bag down the long hall.

"What's in that thing, anyway?" I asked.

"Oh, just a few extra things I thought we'd need," he said, propping it open to expose a mass of mirrors, flash lights, tongue blades and books. "This'll be a cinch."

Inside, our patient — a thin black man — lay deathly still in the first bed, staring overhead at the TV. It was turned off.

Our bottom jaws dropped in unison.

"This looks like it," Stu said after a while, still dumbfounded.

"Good morning Mr. Johnson, I'm *Doctor* Willis and this is *Doctor* Levin." Stu glanced out of the corner of his eye when I emphasized the word "doctor" in my introduction. I glanced back. What the heck, we were going to have enough of a problem as it was convincing Mr. Johnson that we knew what we were doing. We might as well just leave him with the impression that he had been manhandled by two incompetent physicians rather than two kids who didn't even know how to take his blood pressure. That way he wouldn't feel cheated.

"First we need to ask a few questions," Stu said, reaching into his bag and pulling out a long clipboard with a ream of paper clipped to it. "This won't take long, but we gotta get a history concerning your illness."

Mr. Johnson just stared overhead.

"Okay, Mr. Johnson," Stu continued, "what brought you to the hospital?"

Mr. Johnson's bottom lip quivered for a second, but no sound came out.

"You know, what made you think you needed to see a doctor?" Stu asked, with his pencil still poised over the clipboard.

Mr. Johnson let out a faint sigh.

"Did you have a headache or stomachache or something?" I asked, trying to hurry things along.

Suddenly, someone made a muffled sound on the other side of the curtain drawn between the beds.

"Did you have chest pain?" Stu asked.

"You kiddin'? It felt like a elephant sittin' on my chest!" the patient in the next bed yelled from behind the curtain.

"I'm sorry, I'm not asking you," Stu said, already annoyed. "I'm asking Mr. Johnson."

Mr. Johnson was still staring overhead.

"How old are you?" Stu asked.

"Fifty. No, forty. I think," the roommate answered.

Stu ignored the roommate's response. "Now, tell me what's been bothering you," he asked, looking into Mr. Johnson's blank eyes.

"Well, I was walking . . . " the roommate started to say.

"Now wait a minute!" Stu screamed, dashing for the curtain. "I'm not asking you!" He snatched the curtain aside.

In the next bed lay a gray-haired, frail man who looked like a skinny Santa Claus. He was staring out the window, absorbed in something apparently happening just outside.

Stu snatched the curtain back in place.

"Okay now, Mr. Johnson," he said, only slightly more calm, "who brought you to the hospital?"

"Nobody," shot back the answer from Santa.

"How did you get here?"

"I was here already," Santa responded.

Stu glared at the drawn curtain with the fire of Jeremiah in his eyes.

I couldn't control my snickering. I started laughing as Stu stood there, his temple veins bulging, his mouth clamped like a vise.

"Look Stu, maybe we should just go ahead and examine him first. We can get the history later."

For a moment, I thought Stu was going to charge the curtain again and do untold damage to Santa.

Instead, he plunged his hand into his black bag and hoisted out a huge mirror attached to a strap, which he wound around his forehead.

"What do we need that for?"

"Well Rudy, if we're going to do this, let's do it right. The ear, nose and throat docs can see in someone's throat with this thing a hell of a lot better than we can with a pin light."

He flipped a switch on the strap.

A beam of light the size of a car headlamp flashed into Mr. Johnson's face.

Mr. Johnson bolted upright in the bed with wide-open, terrified eyes.

"See," Stu said, chuckling, "it works."

We probed, poked, pushed and listened for several minutes.

"Okay Mr. Johnson," Stu said, "we gotta get your history now."

Johnson was back to his overhead staring.

"As I asked before," Stu continued, "did you have any problems breathing?"

"For two whole days," came the answer from the next bed.

"Were you coughing?"

"Nope."

"Did you sweat?"

"Yep."

"Were you nauseated?"

"Yep."

"For crying out loud!" Stu screamed, dashing for the curtain again, "will you please shut up?!"

This time Santa turned and looked at us with bland gray eyes. It seemed as if he was looking at something in the air between us and him.

"What's with this guy?" I asked.

"I don't know, but he's really wacko," Stu said, seething.

Suddenly, Santa started asking himself questions, then gave himself the answers.

"Did you have chest pain?"

"Yep."

"Where did it hurt?"

"Across the left side."

"Did you vomit?"

"Yep. Broke out in a sweat too."

"What about your breathing?"

"Terrible."

This bizarre scene went on for five minutes.

When I looked over at Stu, he had already started scribbling on his clipboard at a furious pace.

"What are you doing, Stu?"

He didn't answer, trying to catch every word out of Santa's mouth. Mr. Johnson had fallen asleep again.

Twenty minutes later, we lumbered back out to the nurse's station.

"Man! Stu this is ridiculous. What are we going to do now?"

"Look at the chart."

"We're not suppose to do that. If the attending finds out, we'll probably flunk the course."

"Rudy we don't have a choice. It ain't our fault that our patient is out of it, and the guy next door can't keep his mouth shut."

Stu's eyes swept the hall to make sure no attending was around, then he slid the two charts out of the rack.

We slipped into the nurse's lounge and went at it.

Stu was right. Santa—that is, Mr. Beamon—was off keel. He had been transferred from the coronary care unit to recover from a heart attack he had managed to have right in the middle of his admission for acute schizophrenia. His wife had frantically rushed him to the emergency room when he started hearing voices. Apparently he had been quite agitated because of what the voices had told him to do. The result: an extensive myocardial infarction.

"I'll be damned," Stu whispered under his breath.

As it turned out, it was pointless asking Mr. Johnson questions. He couldn't answer.

A couple of weeks before, a blood clot had decided to move up one of his neck arteries and kill off the area of his brain that allowed him to speak. He had an expressive aphasia.

"That's just great," I said, plopping the chart back on the table. "They probably did that to us on purpose. Well, what are we going to do? We're going to look pretty silly in front of the attending with a history from one patient and a physical from another."

Stu and I pictured this humiliating vision of ourselves at the same time. We started laughing.

"Why don't we just change the name," he said, wiping the tear from the corner of his eye when his laughter finally subsided.

"What?"

"Just tell the attending Beamon was our patient."

We quickly exchanged knowing glances, and dashed back down the hall where we poked and probed, this time, on Beamon. When we returned to the room, he was still rambling on about his heart attack.

The attending thought we gave one of the most thorough history and physical exams he had ever heard.

For all of us, the time spent together on clinical rotations seemed to etch lifelong, precious memories of what it took to become doctors. We all fretted, laughed, worried and prevailed during those years. All of us except Jim, who along the way finally decided that life would be happier if he did something else. He got married and went back to Baltimore. For the rest of us, when it was done it was time to drift apart.

Stu headed a little further west. Years later, the East tugged him back home. Every now and then he still dispatches a message to the class of '77 in our medical school magazine. I guess Stu held friendship ties tightly. He and I ended up spending a medical and surgical clerkship together during our junior and senior years. It was great. But before that, we had already known that we were on our way to becoming real docs.

And I knew where I wanted to go. My ultimate goal would be the preeminent halls of the National Cancer Institute at NIH in Bethesda, Maryland.

I never stopped to think that my goal was a heady one for a poor, black kid from Cabrini.

I didn't have to. There were others willing to do that for me.

During my junior and senior years, I rode the wild roller coaster of joy and doubt, success and failure, hope and despair. While every medical school student undergoes similar emotions, my past left me with precious few defenses against the bruising onslaught. My history promised failure. But my task was to defeat my history.

Life would have been easier if there were people around me who could understand that. Instead, there were some who seemed to side with my past in attempting to bring about my defeat. This was especially true during one of my third-year clerkships at Barnes Hospital.

There, the senior ob-gyn resident was as cruel as he was shrewd. Just as life had taught me well, life had taught him well. He was expert in the subtle, destructive application of his own form of injustice.

He was beyond blatant animosity. No harsh words ever crossed his lips. No demeaning jokes. Nothing overt. He never called me "boy."

Far from it.

He was brilliant only in recognizing his own limitations. That brilliance resulted in an insecurity as deeply-rooted as it was well-hidden. To almost everyone else, he was quietly arrogant.

Not to me.

He was brilliant in one other respect. He was able to sense the real abilities in others.

He immediately recognized my ability. As a result, he completely shut me out. Completely.

I was a terrible threat to him. My threat was so real that he had only one defense—deny me all recognition.

For six weeks, I was like a ghost in his presence. I was never acknowledged. My questions were never answered. My name was never spoken.

Not once, not even once, did his eyes meet mine. I was caught only in the sweeping of his cold eyes back and forth from one student to the next in his determined effort to not acknowledge—to never acknowledge—me in their midst, the student who "clearly should not have been there".

That act would have been enough. However, it was compounded by his evaluation of me at the end of the rotation. His one word evaluation? Incompetent.

Incompetent? I was outraged.

"It is not fair!" I shouted at my attending physician during my final evaluation. "The man refused to acknowledge my existence!"

All my emotion came pouring out. The indecency of the resident. He had stymied my desire to learn at every turn.

The attending physician's response?

"These things happen. Once you're a physician, you'll have to deal with all sorts."

"Well, if he is supposed to be a role model," I said, "then this profession is not what everyone makes it out to be."

All that he was willing to do for me was to give me a written exam in order to prove that I was, in fact, "teachable."

"Are you willing to take such an exam?" he asked me.

"Of course," I seethed. I wasn't about to allow such things to stand in my way.

The test required only a few minutes. Having to prove that I was teachable was just one more insult in a lifetime of insults.

I was quite teachable. And I had been taught another lesson. I had come face to face with a most deadly enemy. This enemy had been lurking about for three hundred years, subdued, overt, refining itself, camouflaging itself, pouncing and then reverting to the shadows.

This enemy had destroyed my father and his father before him.

I knew its guises well. I also knew that I would defeat it. I did not enter the fray unprepared. Its children had transformed the battle into a battle of the intellect.

On that battleground, I was more than capable of holding my own.

It was not the words of the attending that uplifted me at times like that but, as usual, those of my mother through her letters.

"Everything will be all right for you, and you will enjoy many happy days. I know your rewards will be many and you will, sooner or later, receive everything you want in life. No one can stop you. God is in the plan. Just keep your mind on your work and your goal, for you are a blessed young man to have such a great opportunity in life. I hope for life's best for you."

I started my cardiology clerkship the following Monday. But I soon found out that like all other blessings, being teachable could also be a curse. It depends on what is being taught.

Doctor White was a retired dentist with end-stage heart disease.

He was also my first patient on my cardiology rotation at Saint Luke's East Hospital.

"Hello, Doctor White," I said, coming to his bed. "I'm Rudy Willis. I'll be taking care of you."

He smiled and extended his hand to me. "It's a pleasure to meet you, son. Of course," he added, eyeing his surroundings. "I'd much prefer it to have been under more pleasant circumstances."

I not only learned that Dr. White had been one of the most popular dentists in the city at the height of his career, but I also learned why. He was a kind man, free with his wisdom and encouragement. His class at Washington University's dental school was always filled.

"So, I understand that you like challenges," he said to me the first day I spoke with him.

He went on to explain that his cardiologist, my Harvard-trained attending physician, had decided that my rapidly developing clinical acumen demanded the challenge of a difficult case.

I was surprised.

"I'll tell you one more thing," Dr. White added. "He's usually not wrong in his assessment of character or ability."

I set about trying to treat his recurrent episodes of worsening congestive heart failure, the result of two heart attacks during his hospitalization. Four weeks later, Dr. White's condition had been stabilized.

"I think we're finally at the light end of the tunnel," I told him.

Drawing a deep, dry breath for the first time in weeks, Dr. White smiled and nodded.

"I'm hoping to have you discharged within the week," I added.

His eyes widened. "Discharged? Really? You think I might be able to finally go home?"

"You can count on it."

A few days later one of the nurses called me to his floor. He had started vomiting uncontrollably the night before. The result of his blood chemistries showed the devastating effect of the lost fluid on his kidney function.

I was stunned when I lifted the page to review his medications. The nurse had misread one of my orders for one of his heart medications, and had given him twice the dose throughout the night.

Doctor White coded in the middle of patient rounds.

"No!" I screamed, rushing to his room as soon as I heard the room number come over the public address system.

No one in that room was willing to give up on Dr. White. We worked and worked to control his intractable, irregular heart beat. In the end, we were defeated.

A day later I had to descend the back, stone stairwell that seemed to lead to the dungeons of Saint Luke's Hospital. I have always wondered why pathology departments have to be in the basement — like radiation departments. It seems that at least in the radiation department we are still trying to cure the curable. But in pathology, we are always forced to look upon the results of our failures.

Several flights below the medicinal odors of the medical wards a long hall disappeared into shifting shadows, its way lit by dusty, naked light bulbs sparsely spaced along its walls. Huge, rust-laden pipes ran its length as it led to a metal door that displayed in bold, white letters "Keep Out." The sick-sweet smell of formaldehyde seeped into the hallway where I now stood.

My attending expected me to attend Dr. White's autopsy. As he stood next to me, I noticed how he kept a watchful eye on me, glancing frequently out of the corner of his eye, as though making sure that I completed my ceremonial christening into our profession without emotional bruising.

As I watched, it reminded me of the weeks spent during my first year in the anatomy lab where, during our feverish learning, we turned nameless remains into a mass of muscles, bones and nerves by the end of the course.

But those were no longer people, at least no longer identifiable. This was different. Here, I knew the soul that had passed through, because I had taken care of it.

I struggled throughout with the conflict between losing a patient and losing a decent, old man who had treated me with respect and kindness, who treated me like a human being.

I wanted to leave the room. To find sanctuary elsewhere. But I knew that there was no sanctuary for me. The only hope for grace I had was lying on the cold, steel pathologist's table.

I lowered my eyes and swore to myself that never again would the care of any of my patients be compromised by inattentiveness — my own or someone else's.

November's pale fallen leaves had been blown away by a chilling December wind. The winter of 1975 had descended on St. Louis with an unusual fury, and its frigid gusts and piles of snow reminded me of Chicago.

I rebounded from Dr. White's death with difficulty. As a result, my performance during the first part my medicine clerkship was mediocre at best.

"I just want this winter to end," I told myself as I stared out my apartment window at the snow. "Things will get better once the winter's over."

That might have been so, but first they were to get worse.

The next evening, the phone rang. I ignored it as I generally did. But it would not stop.

"Hey, Rudy."

"James!" I said, surprised to hear my brother's voice. "How are you?"

"Could be better," he said flatly. "Rudy, Daddy's gone."

I didn't say anything. Gone? Where'd he go? He'd disappeared any number of times for a day, two days, even more.

And yet, I knew this time was different. This time he would not be coming back.

"You'd better come home," James said softly.

I nodded as though James might be able to see me. "Okay."

I searched the handful of faces in the dingy room on North Avenue, next to the L-tracks. The eyes were hooded. There were tears and an almost unfathomable sadness—not just for my father's death, but for a life unlived and unfulfilled.

The felt-covered plywood coffin at the front of the room was all that my mother had been able to afford—just as, thirteen years earlier, she had struggled to provide for the funeral of my Uncle Larry, here in this same, dingy room.

I gazed at the coffin for a long time before I was able to approach.

When I finally did, I looked down at this man, who in spite of his struggles against demons both within and without, had been my father, had cared about me, had sought to instruct me, had tried to provide for me—had loved me.

He had only failed at being the role model he might have wanted to be.

Defeat against unbeatable odds is no shame. It is, however, no privilege either.

When I walked out into the sun and the roar of the steel wheels of the L overhead, my thoughts of my father were commingled with the presentation I was to give the following week — back in St. Louis — to a gathering of medical students, residents and attendings on the medical service.

Before the funeral, I had wanted nothing more than to be relieved of that responsibility. Afterwards, I was determined to deliver that talk. I would do it for myself. I would do it for my father.

When I returned to school, I gave the hour-long presentation—without notes—and followed with an invitation to my audience to engage in an ardent intellectual discussion of the complex pathophysiological aspects of the diseases I had covered.

I wish my father could have been there.

He would have surely been proud. He would have known that, in spite of his personal defeat, there would be some victories . . . well-earned and well-deserved.

My supervising residents praised me for my "omniscient" presentation and gave me a glowing evaluation at the end of the rotation. However, a victory in battle does not win the war.

The attending physician simply refused to recognize my ability and the distance I had traveled to accomplish what I had accomplished. He preferred instead to remember my prior mediocre performance on the service.

This assessment was his inclusion in my reference letter, which was sent to all the hospitals where I applied for residency after graduating from medical school.

I did not hurt from his inability to judge fairly. At that juncture in my life, I took joy only from those who knew precisely where I had come from.

The look on my mother's face when she attended my medical school graduation the following summer was worth the hours, the days, the weeks, the months and years of work.

"He's proud of you, Rudy," she whispered in my ear.

I knew who she was talking about. And I also took note that she spoke of my father in the present tense, as she always did.

My father is with me now, always in the present tense. Though he has finally escaped the harshness of this world, he is even more with me.

Chapter Eleven

She quietly drifted past.

Again she passed, like a perfume-scented wraith, just above and beyond my view as I sat at the nurse's station, huddled over a patient's chart. It was near the end of my pediatric rotation and I was lost in the complicated medical history of a child born a few days earlier. We hadn't figured out what was wrong with baby Ross yet, so the resident had asked me to present her case to our attending physician that morning. But when this prissy nurse glided by a second time, I was compelled to take notice.

She seemed to hesitate for a brief moment as she passed, just long enough for me to mutter a trivial hello.

I had seen her before during the weeks of my clerkship. And, unknown to her, I couldn't help but glance in her direction whenever I got a chance during our morning rounds in the newborn nursery at Barnes Hospital. I had watched her deft handling of the tiny babies who briefly passed through her care on their way to the world outside. I thought that her gentle, skilled care of these little ones revealed a special loving touch, a touch that they seemed to respond to with that primal cooing that tells the world everything is okay.

There, among the plastic bassinets, heat lamps, intravenous tubing and incessant beep of monitors, she moved from child to child, tucking here, patting there, and cuddling at every opportunity. It was as though each of them were her own.

Unknown to me, my fate had already been arranged.

A few days after I had rotated to the service, I was involuntarily adopted by a matriarchal nurse's aid with a stunning resemblance to my Aunt Lois.

"A hard-working young man like you shouldn't be so far away from all those women in the family who used to take care of you," she told me.

So she took it upon herself to make sure that life treated me okay while I was on her service. Each morning she'd make sure that all of the newborns I had to circumcise were neatly lined up at the door of the procedure room. Medical charts were always pulled and stacked for my daily review before rounds started with my resident and attending. And she never let me come through the unit at noontime without slipping an apple, an orange, or a peanut butter sandwich into one of my coat pockets.

Bessie did one other thing. One morning she pulled me aside and told me she wanted me to meet someone.

When I turned around, I found myself gazing into the soft dark eyes of that nurse. A second later I was hooked.

Her name was Angela. She had just completed her undergraduate degree on the east coast and had followed her family to St. Louis, their new home.

It wasn't often that my life stopped for a moment to reveal some semblance of fruition—that is, until Angela came. Although she too had her life demons, the two of us eked out long stretches of time together. We found moments of respite from our grueling profession high above the plain surfaces of downtown St. Louis. There, Stouffers' revolving restaurant ever so slowly pirouetted atop the hotel, forty floors above the hazy street lamps of downtown, unveiling—degree by degree—all that lay beyond this subdued town to which Chicago had led me: the whitewashed pillars of Cardinal Stadium to the south, the shimmering glow of Illinois to the east, and the black, wide-open spaces of Missouri to the west. Stolen weekends were spent lounging on the top of the hills overlooking the quiet, green waters of the lagoons sprinkled here and there in Forest Park.

It was the beginning of a love affair that has lasted for twenty years.

I married Angela a month after graduating from medical school. She subsequently took up my millstones and departed with me when I left St. Louis to go to Kansas City where I had to complete my internship and residency in internal medicine.

113

Those last few weeks of medical school marked another life-changing transition in my life. I had to prepare myself for the turmoil of an intern's life and a new town. Although Kansas City, Missouri was geographically only a slight distance further west, its placid atmosphere placed it light-years away from the raw life I had known in Chicago.

Our tiny two-bedroom apartment occupied the second floor in a cluster of aging buildings on the corner of Paseo and Olivet. The early July predawn light found me speeding westward along Paseo's unkempt boulevard toward Truman Medical Center, the city hospital associated with the University of Missouri School of Medicine. I had been assigned night-call the first night of my internship.

Truman Medical Center sprawled across Holmes Avenue. Its burnt red bricks were so new that one immediately forgot that this was the place where the indigent sought care. The medical school was less than ten years old. It was also novel in another way; it trained its students in only six years after they had completed high school. A select few extremely bright, energetic students were given this opportunity. And they descended upon me—their new intern—with an intellectual fury that was remarkably stimulating.

My two students and I were called to the emergency room that morning to evaluate our first admission.

Mrs. Strong was propped up on a cot along one of the walls. The plastic tubing that blew a stream of oxygen into her air-hungry lungs dangled haphazardly from her neck as she looked about with anxious, frightened eyes. Gathered around her were several family members, who looked on helplessly.

"Mrs. Strong, I'm Doctor Willis," I said, straightening the oxygen tubing, "When did your breathing become so difficult?"

"Well Doc, it really ain't much of a problem," she said in that subtle, southern tone that just barely reminds you that you are in the South. "I kinda ran out of my heart medicine a few days ago."

Actually, Mrs. Strong was having quite a bit of a problem. Even sitting upright I noted that her neck veins were distended with blood all the way up to the angles of her jaws. Her heart couldn't handle the fluid rushing to it from her edematous body. Instead of pumping the fluid

114

out, her heart was letting it back up into her lungs, where it flooded the air spaces and deprived her of oxygen.

"You know, she's been in the hospital so many times," one of Mrs. Strong's daughters said. "Her heart must be in pretty bad shape."

When I listened to Mrs. Strong's lungs with my stethoscope, only the gurgling sound of fluid-logged airways came to my ear. Her heart pounded away, giving off a loud extra thud as her blood made an attempt to return to its chambers. Her legs were so swollen that they looked like they belonged to someone twice her size.

"Let's give her some lasix and some morphine, now please," I ordered the nurse.

When I flipped her chest x-ray onto the view box, it was obvious why she was suffocating. Her heart had swollen to twice its normal size; its flimsy walls bulged outward where they pushed aside her edematous lungs. The amount of oxygen in her blood was even more ominous.

"Your mother has to come into the hospital again," I said.

"Again?" her daughter asked.

"Again."

"But Doc," Mrs. Strong said, "I'm gonna be okay. There's too much to do."

"Mrs. Strong, your heart has just about stopped working. I may have to put you on the ventilator."

"Mama's always lookin' for somethin' to do since daddy died," her daughter explained. "We've told her she can't take care of the farm all by herself. She's got enough of us to take care of her."

Her daughter was right. Gathered around Mrs. Strong's bed were a total of six daughters, two sons and a hoard of wheaten- headed grandchildren.

"Mrs. Strong, we're going to have to take care of you for now," I said.

I was also right. At 2:00am Mrs. Strong coded.

My resident reached her room first. He already had an oxygen mask in place and was now frantically blowing oxygen down her throat.

I straddled her chest and began heart compression. "Get some heart monitor leads on her," I ordered.

The monitor flashed the angry looking saw-toothed pattern of ventricular tachycardia.

"I'm going to shock her!" I yelled. "Stand clear."

Two hundred watts shot from the paddles onto her chest.

She bolted. Her arms flailed upward as though she was attempting to take flight.

"Her pupils are dilating on us," my resident said, still attempting to aim the endotracheal tube into her windpipe.

"I need some lidocaine," I said, resuming the chest compressions.

The resident slipped the tracheal tube in and started massaging the black bag, blowing oxygen into Mrs. Strong's soggy lungs.

"Stand clear," I ordered again.

Again, Mrs. Strong reached for the ceiling, this time as though pleading for mercy.

Suddenly, the monitor's hectic beeps switched to the steady, consoling, beat of a normal heart rhythm.

"We got her back," I whispered, more to myself than to those around me.

The real problem was that Mrs. Strong wasn't completely back. Later, her pupils remained dilated and unmoving as she lay in the intensive care unit, sustained only by the swishing puffs of air pumped into her lungs by the ventilator. Not only that, her EKG revealed a massive heart attack.

"It doesn't look good," I told her daughter.

The family had already begun to gather again. They convened in the tiny waiting room and settled in.

During the next several weeks Mrs. Strong became a permanent fixture on my service. Each morning, my students would present the same unchanging medical status report to the attending. Since it was pretty clear that she wasn't going to wake up soon—if ever—and couldn't breath on her own, we had to perform a tracheostomy to keep her attached to the ventilator . . . Probably forever.

There were many other stirring events during those weeks, but Mrs. Strong's unwavering, lifeless presence weighed most heavily on my mind. This only added to the fatigue of being on call for thirty-six hours every three days. After a while, Angela began to hover over me whenever I was at the apartment. She has continued to hover that way for decades, whenever she senses that life is getting too burdensome for me.

"What have we done?" I asked her one day, not wanting an answer.

"Rudolph, you're a doctor," she said. "Someone always pays a price for whatever is gained."

The problem was that I didn't feel I was the one who had paid the price. It was Mrs. Strong.

Gradually, Mrs. Strong's presence faded into the background while the family waited. They waited for two months.

For me, every third night, the muffled sounds of hospital corridors waited. Outside, the dark stillness would slowly and inevitably settle in, isolating the world of my profession from the everyday cares of those elsewhere. Within those walls, a life could come and go in a moment; it could struggle in a futile effort to become a part of the world outside again, or it could just linger like Mrs. Strong.

Often during those predawn hours I would let those moments of fatigued-respite soften my troubled thoughts about my life, the people I took care of, and the carefree oblivious world outside.

My students were very attentive to Mrs. Strong. Often I noted a group of them at her bedside early in the evening, even when we weren't on call.

One morning, right in the middle of the usual presentation to the attending, Mrs. Strong blinked.

"Did you see that?" the resident asked, shocked.

She blinked twice more. Then, suddenly, she started looking around.

I shoved my way to the head of her bed. Not only was she blinking, she was eyeing—quite disdainfully—all of the tubes leading from her body.

Two days later, Mrs. Strong was sitting up in her bed, munching on a banana and watching TV.

"I got somethin' for you, Doctor Willis," one of her daughters said when I walked into the room.

She handed me a record album. On the cover was a striking picture of her, dressed in a fluffy bright yellow dress, with a fiddle held high on her shoulder. Later I found out that the family had been some of the best fiddle players in Missouri.

"I don't know if you like this kinda music," she said. "But I want you to have this." She had scrawled a large "Thank you" across the front, just above her name.

"My family knows a little about music too," I said, smiling. "Music is music."

I also found out that my students had been more than just a little attentive. Some of them had been vigilant. They later told me that they had prayed for Mrs. Strong. That revelation was surprising, yet not entirely unexpected. I had done all I could for Mrs. Strong. Then one day, out of the blue, something decided it was time for her to get better. I could not explain *why* she got better. Maybe my unspoken faith had also been a spark that kindled the remaining smoldering embers of her life.

A few weeks later, she very slowly walked out the hospital door. And this time she didn't have to come back, at least for the three years that I remained there. In a way, I had made life easier for her.

I still—every now and then—pull out that album to remind me of the victories in this life.

But life had become no easier for my mother. In fact, in many ways it was much more difficult. While I had challenges to vanquish and victories to savor, my mother had only the emptiness of having to face the continued bitterness of life without the silent presence of my father.

Was their married life perfect? Far from it. Ideal was not an option or a reality. But for thirty years, they had carried forward with the mutual understanding of "how things are" on their shoulders. They carried forward certain in their tenacious, unexpressed love for one another, a love which fulfilled their oath at marriage that they would not part until death forced the separation.

"That's the way it's supposed to be," my mother would say later.

After Angela and I got married, she'd undergone surgery to allow her to bear children, and we now were expecting our first child.

My mother came to our apartment in Kansas City to spend a few days with us. I was both excited and fearful of the visit. After all, it would be the first time I would have a chance to spend any length of time with her since I'd left home seven years before.

"Mama," I kept telling her, "you don't have to clean up after us."

"I know, I know," she'd say after making the beds yet again. "But I just feel more comfortable, you know . . ."

"I don't want you to!"

She was surprised by how much emotion was behind my words.

"Mama," I said, coming up to her and leading her to a chair. "I just want you to enjoy yourself. Be our guest. I don't want you to feel that you have to do things like that."

"Rudy, I don't mind doing this. It makes me feel better. And I don't feel any less a guest either."

In some ways, it seemed that she did not want to relinquish the role she had held for so many years, that of mother. However, in other ways, she surprised me by her determination to continue to be more than she had been.

"So much has changed, Rudy," she told me one evening as we sat and enjoyed a cup of coffee. "Too much."

"What do you mean, Mama?" I asked.

"Some of your sisters and brothers, they don't have respect anymore. They . . . they seemed to lose it after your father passed on."

"They're just adjusting," I said.

"Maybe yes and maybe no," she observed. "I like to think that you're right. But I don't know. He was a good man," she concluded softly.

I nodded, averting my eyes from hers. He had been a good man. In spite of everything. Too often we forget that futility too has its grace and heroism. Sometimes just getting up every day and trying—just *trying*—is a heroic act.

Not one day of my life did I ever doubt that I had a father who cared for me, who watched out over me, who expected me to do the right thing.

Yes, he was a good man. Better than that. His absence was a hard blow to my younger brothers and sisters. My mother wasn't able to be both mother and father. With all the things of which she was capable, she wasn't capable of that. She had enjoyed thirty years of not having to be capable of it.

"Rudy," she said, interrupting my thoughts, "I'm taking some courses at the community college."

"Really?" I said, genuinely pleased. "When did you start doing that?"

"Semester before last. I want to get a position as a student teacher at one of the child care centers."

"Mama, that's good. That's real good."

She smiled briefly. "I'll get paid of course. Not very much," she added quickly, "but enough to do something to better my situation, which has been a very unpleasant one."

Her tone was matter-of-fact, but it cut deep into my heart. "Which has been a very unpleasant one." Yes, it had been. I looked at my mother and I saw in her weary body the beautiful, lovely woman she'd been, the woman who had given up a dream in music to marry my father, who had given birth to all of us, who had struggled with us, raised us.

The woman who had watched over me, worrying, holding a dream for me.

There was no bitterness in her voice.

Her eyes were deep and steady as they watched me. "I do not feel any bitterness," she said softly. "I do not have animosity toward no one. Not my children or no one else in this world . . ."

"Mama . . ."

She held up her hand to stop me. She was saying something she wanted to be sure got said.

"See, Rudy, life is filled with trials and errors. No one on this earth is perfect." She sighed. "Mistakes are easy to make. There's always a price needs to be paid."

I remained silent. She was delivering life-sustaining words, and it would be some small mark of my wisdom to take in these words and hold them like the gift they were.

"I hope . . . I hope all my children will always fight for what they want in this life. That is up to them. I believe—*I have to believe*—that with determination, desire and faith they can be anything they want to be.

"It's never too late to try. And keep trying. Never giving up. Keep going until they reach their goals.

"Of course there will be a price to pay, a sacrifice to make. But it's worth it, Rudy. It's always worth it. It's always worth the try.

"I love people, Rudy. You know that. And I dearly love all my children—no matter what they say, no matter what they do, no matter how they act or how they feel about me.

"There is no one else on earth who has a greater love for their children than I do for mine."

She sighed softly. There was a long moment of silence. I wanted to speak but I did not know what to say. It seemed that she was lost for a moment, lost in her thoughts and unable to find a way out.

I felt so inadequate to help her, to help the one person I wanted to help more than anyone else in the world.

"I feel sad," she said finally. "So sad. You know . . . this life, this life . . ."

Those few days that my mother spent with us were among the most fulfilling of my life. I had finally begun to achieve the things professionally that would make her proud. Angela was doing well in her pregnancy, and we were both excited about our first child. And my mother was with me. She was part of my life again.

I felt whole.

But when she returned to Chicago, a familiar void engulfed me. A foreboding. An emptiness.

I felt it for me and I felt it for my mother. I wanted to reach out and protect her. I wanted her to come back and stay with us again . . .

She wrote me a letter filled with reassurances that everything was well. "Rudy," she wrote, "you would be so proud. I received straight A's in my classes. I only have another thirty-six credits until I earn my degree . . ."

I smiled as I read the letter. Then I folded it and tucked it safely along with her many other letters, which I'd saved since she began writing me during my freshman year in medical school.

I brought the sheaf of letters to my face and breathed in deeply of her scent, which lingered on the thin pieces of paper holding her words of love and encouragement.

The void lingered. No matter how I tried focusing on the things that were happening in my life right then and there, I could not make it leave.

On a Sunday evening in August, four weeks after our daughter was born, the phone in our apartment rang. Angela went to pick up the receiver, but I stopped her.

She looked at me curiously. "What's the matter, Rudolph?"

I didn't answer. I just looked at the phone. It rang again. A third time. A fourth.

Slowly, I lifted the receiver and brought it to my ear.

"Rudy . . ."

I lowered my eyes as soon as I heard my brother's voice.

"Hello, James."

"Rudy, Mama collapsed in church..."

I closed my eyes, wishing I could shut out everything around me.

". . . they took her to the emergency room . . ."

My mother died a few hours later from a massive brain hemorrhage. I felt as though there was nothing left.

Angela and I drove to St. Louis to leave our daughter with Angela's mother. Then we headed toward Chicago.

I believe I said only one sentence during the entire three- hour drive. I said, "I will not look in the coffin." That was all. Angela did not say anything in return, and I did not offer any greater comment.

Chicago steamed, but I did not feel the heat. I sat, deadened, at the corner of our bed, gazing out the window of our hotel at the pale waters of Lake Michigan.

I waited.

"Rudolph, we'd better get started."

I did not answer.

"Rudolph," Angela said, a few moments later.

My eyes remained fixed on the lake.

She placed her hand on my shoulder. "Come on. It's time."

We joined the small caravan forming in front of Johnson's store-front funeral parlor on North Avenue.

I repeated to myself over and over that I would not look upon my mother's face in death. Like a mystical chant.

I had become convinced that if I were to look upon her as I had looked upon my father and my Uncle Larry, my life would end. I was determined to exercise that bit of will in order to be able to survive.

A few years later, that same determination kept me from gazing down at the face of my baby brother, Steven, in death.

My love for all of them was simply too great.

"Go on," my sister, Yvonne, urged me when Angela and I arrived at the funeral parlor. "Go on and see Mama before they close the coffin."

I shook my head. "I can't, Yvonne."

She looked at me with a confused expression on her face. "What do you mean, you can't? She's your mama."

How could I explain to her that she was asking me to do the one thing in the world that was impossible for me to do?

"She looks good, Rudy. You don't have to be afraid. You know," she went on, "I bought her the finest casket they had."

They slowly eased my mother's casket down the stairs, letting it hesitate only a moment when it reached me. Then, as the coffin passed through the door, the sun's rays skimmed its metallic surface. It changed to pale blue—the color of a cloudless sky.

I lowered my eyes, realizing that the most beautiful thing that my mother ever possessed was the casket in which she was buried.

Angela guided me back out to the car. I drove mechanically, my eyes straight ahead. I pulled into place in the small motorcade, which then moved forward slowly, reverently. We rolled through stop signs and red lights. We rolled through Old Town. The very same Old Town to which I had ventured endlessly during the days of my youth.

There was an unreal sense to how everything was unfolding. The children laughing and shouting on the street could have been me — were me.

How the streets of Chicago bustled that day, filled with carefree people. I could hear the voices of the people on the street, but they seemed to come from a great distance.

"Rudy, toss me the ball, man!"

"Rudy, you ain't never gonna be good at stealin'."

"Rudy, Mama says we got to get back soon."

"Rudy, Mama says . . ."

123

Rudy. Mama.

"Rudolph, are you all right?"

I turned and saw the concerned look in my wife's eyes.

"Yes," I told her. "I'm fine. Just fine."

I wondered if any of the people on the street could possibly grasp the connection of their lives to our lives . . . to the lives all around them.

The drive to Burr Oak Cemetery seemed as long as the drive from St. Louis. I kept my eyes dead ahead, on the hearse carrying the pale blue coffin.

We passed through the far southern suburbs, past fine, manicured lawns and picture-window brick houses, houses like my mother said we would live in someday.

"Someday has come and gone, Mama," I whispered.

"What?" Angela asked.

I simply shook my head.

My sadness deepened when we drove past the huge, steepled Lutheran church. I knew this was the end of the line. Beyond the church sprawled a grassy-hilled cemetery filled with a sea of slate-gray monuments, garish monuments, two-story high monuments—all crying out the absurdity of vanity.

A polished, six-foot high black iron fence surrounded the four-block cemetery. Even here, even in death, there were neighborhoods, and my mama was not to reside in the best of them.

We slowly made our way to the single gate that opened to my mother's place of rest. Foot-high headstones identified gravesites. The grass was neatly trimmed, with carefully planted clumps of yellow, white and pink flowers along the gravel walkways.

But even this lovely place was not to be my mother's final abode. No. We continued on, driving down a twisting road to the back of the cemetery where the grass disappeared and sandy dirt covered the ground.

This was the poor neighborhood. Flat. Barren. Sad land, with only a scattering of wooden sticks to mark the graves, to let a visitor know that this, too, was a place of final rest for people once loved in the world.

A neighborhood of the poor. People as lost in death as in life.

As I followed along after my family, my eyes searched desperately over the dusty soil, looking in vain for some sign—any sign—of my father's grave. But he had already been lost in the sea of unmarked and unremarkable dirt.

Death had found him a sanctuary as unkind as life.

When we finally stopped, it was as if we had stopped in the middle of a parking lot. We stood on hard and gravelly ground.

"How out of place Mama's beautiful casket will be here," I thought to myself.

I stood still as James, Ronald, Brian, and Steven lifted my mother's casket from the hearse and gingerly positioned it over the hole which was to accept her.

Without warning, without a sound, without the ache that had become my constant companion in this world, tears sprang suddenly to my eyes. They flooded my view as my mother's pale blue casket slowly descended into the ground.

As a child, when sleep escaped me late into the night, I would attempt to sort out the events in my family. Often I could hear my mother softly singing through the thin bedroom wall. During the daylight hours, she tended to hum. But during the night, when the darkness wrapped its sympathetic and full silence around our apartment, she would sing full songs, songs that seemed to bring out the deep pain that lived at the soul of her being.

She sang most nights, singing soft hymns to her children who found no sanctuary in the night, to her children who could find no sleep until her voice carried them there.

Even now, the dark nights are strangers to me, because of the silence that has replaced her voice.

Chapter Twelve

The gathering at my mother's funeral was the last time we came together as a family. We all were there, except Bernitta. I always wondered who—if anyone—told her that her mother was gone. All of us, in our own ways, had to absorb one more loss, one more deprivation. It left telltale signs in each of our lives.

Yvonne developed a frantic edge to her stout character. She became a teacher, married her high school sweetheart, and spent the next twenty-five years in Chicago trying to forget the past in which she still lived.

Ronald became a master mechanic. But one day, just before he turned thirty, his anger unexpectedly erupted. Only the luck of his victim saved him from becoming a murderer. He survived that event, and later learned the value of both his faith and his own family.

Brian became the Protector of Steven, our baby brother. He watched over Steven as I had watched over him and Ronald, but it was not enough. Steven became an alcoholic before he was barely twenty. One day Steven was found seizing in a dilapidated Chicago tenement. He died before he could ever use any of the gifts passed to him by my mother or father. It was Brian alone who found a way to have him buried.

Andrea became a nurse and the single parent of two children. She later became a counselor for drug abusers. She developed a disturbing resemblance to my mother, a haunting reminder of the face I could not look upon in death.

Kimberly became the mirror image of my mother in another way. She brilliantly completed three years of college only to later have her goals annihilated by giving birth to ten children.

Shinette, my baby sister, became a preacher. The preacher that I thought I should have become.

But James. My brother James.

The years that followed rapidly turned his hair gray. He continued to roam. Although he had survived both Vietnam and Cambodia, he still had problems surviving the life given to us. He became a psychologist after a passionate effort to join the FBI. But over the ensuing years his life could be calmed only by alcohol. He did manage to marry and raise a family. I would not see him again after he helped lower my mother's coffin into her grave.

After my mother's funeral, I returned to Kansas City. There I realized that I had lost one other thing I cherished in life—my passion for learning. The uncontrolled, fiery enthusiasm that had carved a nearly insatiable curiosity had flickered, then gone out.

It seemed I was no longer a student, the role that had defined me and my life.

I performed my hospital duties with mechanical efficiency, but without heart. I was, I realized, slowly allowing myself to mentally die.

"Rudy," I told myself, "this is what you will do. You will walk these halls until you have walked them one year, ten years, or more, until you have slowly and finally wound down to nothing."

I couldn't let that happen.

I did not so much look for rebirth as for sanctuary when I turned to the legions of scientific data and papers on the mechanisms of cell regulation, gene control and the processes of cancer. I found comfort in the reams of information. This was the language of the mind that spoke so clearly to me. It had always done so.

However, something happened as I sought this sanctuary. My mind made unconscious leaps. Connections. Questions. Answers. Possibilities.

I began to play mentally with these possibilities. Slowly, they evolved into something more formal.

The result of my deliberation, of my attempt simply to hide in safety, was a theoretical model for gene regulation which attempted to explain a host of little-understood biochemical, viral, chemical, hormonal and cancer-causing events in the genes of humans.

When I submitted my model for publication, the editors of some of the scientific journals had difficulty conceiving the validity of the theoretical basis of my article. In spite of that problem, the article was accepted for publication and was subsequently noted by researchers at the National Institutes of Health. As a result of the attention of one or two of these researchers, I was offered a position as a Clinical Oncology Fellow at the National Cancer Institute in July, 1984.

On a hot Friday evening Angela, my daughter and I headed for Washington DC.

Highway 70 rolls eastward with the same abandon as it does to the west. It wanders back across the moping brown waters of the Mississippi, subtly shying away from Chicago while seeking a more genteel southern route through the patchwork countryside of southern Indiana.

Then it rushes northward, zigzagging its way to the outskirts of West Virginia before it pokes a mile-long hole through the side of the Allegheny Mountains. On the other side, it climbs to the craggy rims of Pennsylvania's grassy hilltops before making a prolonged descent into the fields of Maryland. There, reverently, it finally eases past Gettysburg, ending its journey in a smooth, straight path that hurries into Washington DC.

The clinical center of The National Institutes of Health stands like a grand hotel.

Saving Grace on a Less Traveled Road

Bethesda Maryland hugs the northwest boundary of Washington's roving, crisscrossed city landscape. Its serene, cultivated, tree-lined roads stand in stark contrast to Washington's furiously crowded avenues and pretentious displays of self-worth. The wise founders of NIH chose its site well.

In 1887 NIH was little more than an idea. It was called the Hygienic Lab then, and occupied the Public Health Institution's Marine Hospital on Staten Island. Three years later it was transported to Washington, DC, where it became the Public Health Institution and began to establish its role in health issues and train local doctors in dealing with epidemic outbreaks. It was funded by Congress for the first time in 1930, when it was named The National Institutes of Health. It became America's—and the world's—premier research facility for the study of diseases in man.

In 1937 NIH began to specialize, and the National Cancer Institute became its firstborn. It moved one final time, to Bethesda, setting the scene for medical history.

Hidden beneath a mile-long cluster of aging oaks is a row of two-lane streets that split from Bethesda Avenue, all heading in the same direction. To the unknowing, they appear to be little more than entrances to dead-end streets. But they all lead to a spacious plot of grassy land only a half a block away. Here, rising fourteen stories above Bethesda's tranquil roads, towers the Clinical Center of NIH.

It stands like a grand hotel, stories above the treetops. In all directions, manicured, lush green grass spreads out into the surrounding thirty-acre campus. Low-rise rectangle buildings sprinkle the quiet lawns, each numbered in the order they were erected over the prior fifty years. Within these reside the laboratories of some of the country's best scientists. Their halls still echo the names of Nobel Laureates like Kornberg and Nirenberg.

Over the years, NIH became the gatekeeper for any post-doctorate graduate with any plans to become noteworthy in his field. The competition to get there was furious. Becoming a Clinical or Research Associate at NIH sometimes became the only precondition for potential academic greatness.

In 1965 an energetic physician joined that tradition. His name was Robert Gallo.

The clinical achievements within the Cancer Institute remain groundbreaking decades later. The early work of Vincent DeVita led to the first truly curative cancer regimen and set the pattern for the development of other promising drugs. This was accomplished through the use of experimental treatment plans. For this reason, patients are sent to NIH from all over the country. We Clinical Fellows were responsible for the care of the patients on these treatment plans.

I noticed that when Gary walked into the clinic he stood to one side at the check-in desk for several minutes before he cautiously came forward. Under one arm he held a large manila envelope; it bulged from the weight of the material stuffed inside. He had been sent by his doctor in New York City.

Gary was my first clinic patient and I was looking forward to entering a patient on one of our cancer treatment protocols. The nurse handed me the envelope while she readied him in one of the examination rooms.

The records inside the envelope told a harrowing story. Several months ago Gary had a chill. Nothing alarming, just a brief wave of coldness that set his teeth chattering. A few days later, his muscles began to ache. It felt as if he had the flu. The problem was that it was in the middle of the summer and this "flu" didn't go away. After the lymph glands began to swell in his neck, he received several weeks of antibiotics. It didn't help.

Then the diarrhea started, followed by drenching sweats, sweating so intense that he placed plastic over his mattress at night instead of attempting to replace his soggy bedding.

One day while sitting at the desk in his office, he stopped breathing. Gary ended up on a ventilator with pneumonia in both of his lungs. He had an infection with an organism to which all of us are exposed everyday, but the problem was that something had completely destroyed his body's resistance. The result—several months later—was the frail, wisp of a man who now sat before me, and whose vacant stare confirmed the merciless damage already done.

His story was not unlike hundreds told in our medical journals over the prior two years. It started in San Francisco and Los Angeles, then New York and Miami. By 1981 it was clear that the United States and the world were beginning to learn about one of the most terrifying diseases in history. Around the world, the human consciousness would echo with memories of the bubonic plague—the Black Death. But this disease was to be different in even a more terrifying way. The infectious agent inserted itself into the genes, where it could replicate at will—as long as its victim survived. Unfortunately, it was unforgiving. And no one survived.

One other unusual thing had happened to Gary. He noticed strange, purplish nodules spreading over his skin. A biopsy of one of these had revealed a rare cancer virtually never seen in healthy young men. It was for this reason that he had been sent to us.

"Been kinda difficult?" I asked, trying to put him at ease, hoping he would not share with me all of the terror. He sat on the examination table, looking back at me through sunken eyes.

"Hellish would be more appropriate, Doc."

He looked starvation-thin, and much of his skin was covered with reddish-blue nodules. Although he was only twenty-five years old, his youth was lost in the folds of thin, sallow skin sagging beneath his eyes.

"Gary," I said after completing my exam, "your biopsy shows Kaposi's Sarcoma. We have several treatment plans here and you would qualify for one of them."

"That's fine, but what are we going to do about the rest of me?"

At first I thought his question was touched with cynicism. Then I realized the full weight of its seriousness. He was looking for hope. Any hope.

"Gary, we're not even sure yet," I said, trying not to sound too pessimistic, "what's happening to people who get this disease."

"You know," he said, looking lost, "that's too bad, because I don't think I can wait very long."

He was right. The next day he was to return to the clinic following the results of tests ordered the day before. Instead, the clinic nurse got an angry call from one of the emergency room doctors in a nearby hospital.

Gary had been found unconscious in his hotel room and rushed to the emergency room, where they attempted to resuscitate him. Later, when the hospital realized he had AIDS, everyone there was furious. Our clinic nurse politely held the phone to her ear and patiently endured one tirade after another for nearly twenty minutes. After all, we were the National Institutes of Health and were expected to be civil even with the most uncivil public.

They came from every sector of the campus: from the laboratories of biochemistry, from cell physiology and immunology, from the laboratories of tumor biology, and from the laboratories of virology. The flow of white-coated NIH researchers and physicians was steady and relentless; a stream of the country's best scientific investigators poured through the double doors of the majestic auditorium in the Clinical Center. A week after I had seen Gary in the clinic, we all went there to hear Dr. Robert Gallo tell us about the new virus his lab had found floating in the blood stream of the patients with this new frightening disease.

Already there were whispers of the significance of this discovery, and there was growing reverence among researchers all over the country for the man who stood before us.

At the podium stood an energetic speaker whose words evoked an aura of restrained urgency. His lab's prior accomplishments could not be ignored. For years he had sought to prove the existence of human viruses that could cause cancer, viruses capable of changing their own genes into a form that allowed them to become a part of a cell's DNA. His lab had found two of these viruses. One caused leukemia.

He saw similarities between the consequences of infection by his leukemic virus and the disease that devastated the body's resistance in people like Gary. Early on he was convinced that the cause of this new disease was an infection, and that the infection was caused by a virus.

Two years prior, his lab used a protein made in the body to stimulate blood cells obtained from these patients and began to look for evidence of the genes of this new virus hidden within the blood cell's genes. At the same time, he attempted to identify the activity of an important protein that had to be produced by this new virus to allow its genes to merge with those of the cell.

A year later, the blood from a patient who had received a blood transfusion offered its secret. A highly magnified picture of the cells displayed strange particles budding from the surface of the blood cells. By mixing the blood of several patients together, he was able to infect a self-growing clone of blood cells with the new virus.

In May of 1984, when I arrived at NIH, a flurry of articles published by Robert Gallo appeared in the scientific journals. These articles demonstrated production of the virus in the lab, showed how the virus could be identified in infected patients, and told the world what the virus was made of. Already, many had admitted that this work was the work of a future Nobel Prize winner.

This work was so significant that the Secretary of Health had been forced to hold a news conference before its publication to inform an anxious America of the achievement. Afterward, news articles in every major paper in the country echoed the breakthrough . . . "The probable cause of AIDS has been found . . . Can be produced and blood test available."

But it was not this that drew me to Robert Gallo. What fascinated me was the nature of this microbe—its capacity to create such ruinous havoc. It immediately became clear to me that such power could only be achieved by usurpation of the normal control of our very genes. This was novel, awesome and frightening. To decipher the complexity of the events involved in this process would be a formidable challenge, the kind of challenge in which I needed to be absorbed.

When I left the auditorium that morning, I knew that I would become a molecular biologist in the laboratory of Robert Gallo.

While growing up, life had been uncompromising in its determination to teach me the lessons that would guide me through its arduous offerings. Life cared not for my lack of understanding of why things had to be the way they were; it offered no explanations; it offered no apologies. But it did offer, ever so gracefully, the right portions of heartache. This it had done carefully and knowingly. After I arrived at the Cancer Institute, I knew why.

A flood of stricken people poured into the clinic over the following year. They came with the ravage of other kinds of cancers. They too had been sent to seek any miraculous potions we may have concocted for their terminal diseases. More often than not, the outcome of our efforts was little better than the flip of a coin or the flight of a winged-prayer. Yet, in the tradition of the Institute we piled protocol upon protocol, as though the sheer number of our treatment options would make people better and take away the untold suffering from their diseases.

During my year as a Clinical Fellow I learned much about cancer. I learned even more about the character of the soul. As the weeks turned into months, I realized that the outcome of what we did to our patients often had nothing to do with what chemicals we poisoned their bodies with or how many jolts of radiation we gave them. The outcome often, and undeniably, seemed to tether itself to the firmness of their faith—faith in an entity capable and willing to let them survive. The passage of those who had nothing to which to cling was often grievous, both for them and for me.

This is the way it was for my patients then, and this is the way it would always be after I became a cancer doctor. But more than this. If I learned anything, it was the reality that, in the end, life evens out any prior inequities in suffering. Often it does so only in the end—when it's time to die. This wisdom life offered to me during that year, before it was time to set aside the care of my patients.

Building 31 stood in the middle of a grassy field, protectively surrounded by a gathering of two-story, bleached buildings. Unlike many of the other buildings on the campus, building 31 rose above its surroundings. Its entrance opened into a large paved plaza with a wide row of steps that led to the parking area. It looked like a tiny replica of the United Nations. But its structural uniqueness is not what distinguished it from all the other laboratory buildings. What made it noteworthy was the Laboratory of Tumor Cell Biology, which resided on its upper level. It was where the AIDS virus had been isolated.

During my clinical year at the Institute, Gallo's lab had not only cloned the virus, but also completely sequenced its genes. In July of 1985, the lab was well on its way to understanding and describing the function of the genes in this minute, deadly microbe. Genes with names like TAT, REV and POL. The lab had deciphered its structure and had begun to suggest how it achieved its horrific destruction in those it infected.

Saving Grace on a Less Traveled Road

The door to Steve Joseph's lab was hidden among the rows of boxes and freezers that lined the hall, and its half panel of glass was smothered beneath a swarm of notes taped and pasted in every niche of remaining clear space. Inside, a lanky, bearded investigator was leaning over his bench, concentrating on the tiny plastic tubes in buckets of ice scattered around him.

When he looked up, a brief smile came to his face, sharpening his keen, dark eyes even more.

"I'm Rudy Willis," I said, extending my hand. "I'm the new Fellow assigned to your lab."

"Well, Rudy we've been waiting for you," Steve said, slipping off one of his gloves and waving at the bench across from him. "We got an area for you already set up."

Shelves four tiers high lined the walls of the tiny lab. Each was engulfed by a sea of test tubes and flasks, mountains of jars containing salts and acids and colorful liquids. The dull marble workbenches seemed to sag under the weight of large vats of water and centrifuges. The air smelled of both the sweet aroma of benzene and the acrid odor of sulfu-

Building 31 at NIH, where I worked on the AIDS virus.

135

ric acid. It immediately reminded me of the years I had spent in Welk's lab. That memory sparked a forgotten enthusiasm.

"We've been kinda busy around here," Steve said, slipping a tiny tube out of the ice bucket and squirting a blue dye into it. "Actually, kinda crazy would be a better description."

"Yeah, the number of papers the lab published last year was amazing," I said.

"Well, what do you think you want to do for the next couple of years?" Steve asked, squirting dye into the rest of the tubes.

"I'm interested in the viral mechanisms that cause cancer to develop in these patients, particularly their skin cancer."

"That's a difficult one," Steve said. "You know, I spent a lot of time looking for the gene footprints of viruses other than this AIDS virus in the tumor cells from patients and found nothing. Maybe you're right."

I realized what it was about Steve that was likable. It was the way he responded to rookie investigators like myself, considerately weighing the value of their opinions. This was encouraging, considering the fact that my training as a physician had nothing to do with the kind of complex, basic science research that Ph.D.'s like himself perform daily.

"The problem is," Steve continued, "that we're in a middle of a critical period in all of the work we've done. As you know, we've identified many of the genes in the virus, including its polymerase, necessary for its replication."

"You mean the POL gene?" I asked.

"Right. Sam Broder's group is looking at possible inhibitors for potential drug development already. If we could clone the polymerase gene, it would allow us to set up an assay to test how good the drugs work against the virus before clinical trials are started."

"I see, it's a matter of priority."

"I'm afraid so. Maybe you can get started on cloning the polymerase for us. Then, hopefully you can get around to looking at a few of the other genes like TAT to see exactly what other role it plays in the virus."

I considered his suggestion.

"Don't worry," Steve said. "I'm going to teach you all the techniques you need to get started. Then you're on your own."

While we were talking, two other junior investigators walked into the lab.

Volker was from Germany. He immediately strolled over with the kind of proud, upright stride that declared confidence. "Welcome!" he said in a deep German accent.

The other researcher gracefully followed. His jet-black, hefty mustache and thin, inky hair reminded me of blazing suns, swirling sands and mystical tales. He was from Persia. "My name's Resa," he said, holding out his hand. "I hope we can work on a project together."

I soon found out that Gallo's group of investigators hailed from nearly every part of the world. Across the hall, Guo had made his way there from China; in the lab next to him, Takanaka worked; next to Steve, Sarin's lab stood; down the hall people hailed from France. I was now truly a long way from Cabrini. I wondered what they would have thought if I could have somehow explained to them from where I had come.

Later that morning Steve took me over to Gallo's office.

I was right. Gallo was energetic. As we walked through the door, he jerked his head up from the pile of papers on his desk to which he had been attending. A brief look of surprise flickered in his eyes, then a faint smile settled around his lips.

"I hope Steve is taking care of you," he said, leaning over his desk and shaking my hand firmly.

I had heard much about this now-famous man—how he had come to NIH as a physician twenty years before and become a molecular biologist by force of will and an insatiable enthusiasm for his work. Like others, I had heard how the death of his only sibling from leukemia affected his childhood, and in turn initiated the spark that led him to the quest to identify the first cancer-causing virus. But I had also heard the whispers of other things. Rumors and hints that things were not all as they should be in his lab. Suggestions that the virus identified in his lab belonged to someone else. But then, these were only rumors.

Our subsequent encounters were frequent but brief. It would take some time for me to sort through the morass of accusations surrounding this mysterious man.

As it turned out, my first task was as simple as it was complex. The genes of the virus had already been inserted into the DNA of plasmids, entities capable of replicating their own DNA. Since the virus' DNA had already been sequenced, I knew the regions that contained the polymerase gene, and I knew specifically the exact gene code at the region where this gene was inserted into the virus' DNA. All I had to do was to snip out the polymerase gene with a group of natural enzymes that would cut the DNA at exactly the right place. Then it would be necessary to extract the cleaved gene from the rest of the virus' DNA by letting it move through a bed of gel at very high voltage. Using other kinds of enzymes that bind DNA, I would have to reinsert just the polymerase gene back into a plasmid capable of replicating the gene and making the protein that comes from the gene. This would allow Sam Broder to test the effect of one of his new drugs–AZT—on the protein.

My methods were simple and logical—that is, on paper. It didn't take long to realize that DNA, laboratory equipment, chemicals, and enzymes don't always do what they are told, no matter how logical the approach. Gels fell apart; enzymes snipped where they pleased; genes reunited where they weren't suppose to; and when I did isolate the gene, the amount was so paltry that it seemed to disappear in the test tube that supposedly contained it.

This went on for months. All that salvaged the situation were my competitors at another research lab, whose equipment, enzymes and gels *did* work.

My first defeat in the competitive world of research was stinging but not disheartening. Although I had not completed my project adequately, I learned the techniques that would eventually lead to a much greater triumph. I also learned that this world's achievements were as hard to come by as the one I grew up in.

After we moved to Washington, my wife continued to work as a pediatric nurse. We were able to buy a small house and begin the process of becoming a family. But there was one last thing that I also learned during that first year in the lab: the work was intense and life consuming. In a moment, the seemingly trivial concerns of the world outside the lab would fade into the background, leaving behind the endless, silent days and nights at the bench, where I always seemed to be only one step away from success.

Resa was very supportive during those months, often suggesting new approaches and additional refinements in my techniques. When he spoke, I listened. He had come to the lab by way of Oxford, and the results of his research attested to the fact that, in the lab, his hands were golden. One day he came to my bench, where I sat, still despondent over my failure.

"Rudy, how goes it?" he asked from behind his thick mustache.

"You know Resa," I said, "this business is fickle. One moment you're about to do what hasn't been done before, the next moment somebody else is telling everyone how they've already done it. It stinks."

"Well welcome to the club of the disenchanted," he said, with an exaggerated sour look on his face in an attempt to make me laugh.

"Just the same, it probably feels a lot better when your name is on that published paper, and not someone else's."

"That's not the point, Rudy," Resa said, looking more serious. "It's the beauty of the work that counts." He was silent a moment. "And the toil you put into it."

Resa's last comment echoed over and over again in my head. He was right. Although research was unpredictable, so was life. And, like everything else that's worth achieving in life, it's the value that you give to the toil that uplifts even the seemingly most trivial goal to a level of nobility.

"Look," Resa said, interrupting my thoughts, "why don't we do some work together?"

"What did you have in mind?"

"Forget about the polymerase gene. It's not important and wasn't worth the trouble."

"That's ridiculous, Resa. The virus can't even insert itself into human DNA without its polymerase gene."

"Yea, but the virus can't produce its parts without the TAT gene. I tell you, this gene, if altered, will shut the virus down completely. Now that's important."

Resa had a point. We had learned a lot about this AIDS virus. We had identified all of its genes—or so we thought—and we were pretty sure of what role each gene played in the survival of the virus. But there were many, many more unanswered questions about this magnificently mysterious microbe.

"If we mutate regions of the genes," Resa continued, "we will better understand how we can stop its replication."

"There's more to it than that," I said, now understanding his point. "If we can identify the important regions of the TAT gene by making those regions defective, we will know which portions of the TAT protein are critical for its function. Maybe drugs can then be developed which will bind to these regions and shut down TAT."

Resa and I were silent for a moment, letting the significance of my last comment linger in the air.

"Not only shut down TAT," Resa finally said, "but shut down the virus too."

That was all that needed to be said.

Resa and I approached our problem in roundabout fashion. The role of DNA in any organism is to provide the blueprint for the production of proteins. And the three-dimensional structure of these proteins depends upon the interaction of its amino acid links. Biochemistry had taught me how certain amino acids in proteins are capable of making stronger bonds with each other than with other amino acids along the protein's chain. It is this type of amino acid interactions that tug and tease parts of the protein into a spiral, globule or loop. This process results in the development of unique structural areas in the protein—areas critical for the protein's normal function. Since there is a direct correspondence between the sequence of bases in the DNA and the sequence of the amino acids in its protein, all we had to do was to carefully select regions in the DNA that coded for the critical regions in its protein product. By mutating these regions in the DNA, we would cause a defective protein to be produced by the virus. This would result in the virus' inability to reproduce itself.

Resa and I identified the regions of the TAT protein we thought were important for its normal function. Then, by two different techniques, we went about the business of shutting down the AIDS virus.

Chapter Thirteen

Washington DC's lukewarm days seem to merge imperceptibly into a brief, frigid fall before changing into the crisp, cherry-blossom mornings of spring. The flow of months is unnoticed except by a reposed eye and attentive spirit. But it is not only the change of season that goes unnoticed there. Changes of fortune are of equal disinterest. For there is a level of indifference and lack of substance that is particular to Washington. It is a place where authoritative, embattled souls cling ever so tenuously to fleeting power.

From a distance, all seems well. From above, through the thickened, glazed panes of an airplane's window, the straight paths of Washington's thoroughfares, like paved spokes, all seem to flow in orderly fashion to the capital's hub—a perfect Ferris wheel of streets and roads viewed from aerial heights.

But this deceptive sense of order is banished in a moment by the hurried and harried traffic below. There, streets end without a warning or a cause, interrupted by blocks of haphazardly placed buildings, only to reappear miles away—often headed in another direction. Street names are replaced by just a letter of the alphabet, or a number, used over and over again. North, South, East and West are obliterated from the map by roads that run at the oddest angles and in wandering paths.

Washington DC is not what it first seems to be.

Often I wondered if Washington's sheer confusion of direction was responsible for the disorientated, aimless lives led by some of those who lived there. A frenzy permeated the air, boldly, recklessly, tossing to and fro the unstable dreams of many. And when these dreams perished—as they often did—there was nothing left for the dreamer but the comfort of a pretended success, a success which had little more substance than the puffiness of a cloud.

Saving Grace on a Less Traveled Road

I was thankful that my dreams had been brought with me when I moved to Washington, dreams unburdened by the apparent worldly shallowness of spirit existing there. For this reason, not having a life outside of the lab was, at first, not a lost chance at all. It was a gracious pardon.

Resa's and my work had gone well. Gallo regularly had his investigators gather to present the status of their research. Several months after Resa and I began our project we, like our colleagues, were expected to show the fruits of our labor. Nearly two years had passed since I had attended Gallo's presentation to an admiring audience. Much had happened in those two years. My research skills had improved at a dizzying pace, and I was well on my way to making a reasonable contribution to an important project. I should have been thrilled, but uneasiness began to overshadow any joyful thoughts about my success. This uneasiness had nothing to do with my work.

Resa had chosen a more skilled, elaborate way of achieving the mutation of the TAT gene. Mine was unsophisticated and elegantly simple. I utilized a set of nucleases—enzymes that cut DNA at specific sites—to remove small sections of the TAT gene. Then I ligated the gene back together with a different set of enzymes. This process results in a minute alteration in the gene's sequence, and in turn, causes the virus to produce an altered protein. After making a series of altered TAT genes, I could later test the effect on the activity of the TAT gene.

Over the prior months I had made several mutations which only slightly affected the TAT gene. But I knew which region of the gene probably had to be altered to completely shut down the virus' ability to replicate.

One late summer evening I, as usual, returned to the lab to look at the DNA patterns created by my most recent mutations. I turned off the light in the Dark Room and flipped on the switch of the ultraviolet light box.

The gel slab containing my DNA burst into the mysterious, orange glow emitted by the ethidium bromide-stained DNA, reflecting off my face and bathing the tiny room in a reddish-yellow flare of light.

There, in the midst of pieces of glowing DNA, lay the pattern of the mutant I was looking for.

When I tested it for gene activity, there was none. Absolutely zero. The TAT gene had been completely turned off.

We gathered in the large room reserved for the periodic review of the work being performed in all of the laboratories within Gallo's department. These meetings, depending upon the quality of the work presented, could be the arena for the start of an outstanding career or the sepulcher where tarrying work and its investigator met a merciful end. The response to one's work could range from sanctification to annihilation.

When it came time for me to make my presentation, Gallo got up from the long table at the front of the room and made his way back to where I was sitting.

"Rudy, are you ready to go," he asked, "or would you like to wait until next time?"

"I might as well do it now," I told him.

I was surprised that he had stopped the proceedings just to make sure I felt comfortable with how my work was going—before I had to stand before a room filled with some of the best researchers in the country. Over the prior several months, my ambivalent feelings about what had happened in the lab thwarted my ability to make a final judgement about Gallo. Behavior like this only confused me.

Resa and I had decided that I would present the theoretical basis for our work and the method I had chosen to use. He would then present some preliminary data.

In the middle of my presentation, I noticed a small disturbance at the table where Gallo and his senior investigators sat. Gallo's secretary was leaning over the table and whispering something into his ear. A brief, pained look spread down his face then disappeared. Then he leaned over and started an animated conversation with the person next to him.

Like the expanding, fiery rings of a nuclear bomb, the commotion at the table spread down each end and then into the first row of people in the audience before it resumed its disruptive surge into the room. Brief outbursts started to come from Gallo's table.

When I returned to my seat, everyone was already heatedly discussing the problem. A reporter at the *Chicago Tribune* had just published an article on the lawsuit filed by a French research group, accusing Gallo of using the AIDS virus—first isolated by them—without permission to produce the HIV test.

The rest of our planned sessions were totally disrupted by the news.

"We can't let this sort of thing disrupt our work," Gallo said to one of the investigators involved in the early work on the virus.

The investigator bolted angrily to his feet, only a few chairs away from where I now sat.

A singeing orb of agitation swelled from where he stood, engulfing those of us nearby in its blistering path.

"I think we should explain some things—" he began.

"We've already explained enough!" Gallo shot back.

The session dissolved into pockets of irritable conversations until everyone drifted away.

The weeks and months that followed brought with them not disruption, but a slow erosion of morale, leaving behind troubled minds and unsure hearts. Slowly, the old faces in the department began to disappear as researchers began to seek higher ground elsewhere, fleeing in the face of the inevitable flood of world scrutiny. Those who did not leave immediately took out their frustrations on each other.

One night I returned to the lab to the sound of smashing glass, yells and slamming doors.

"*Du bist nicht gut!*" (You are no good!), Volker was yelling as he glared down the hall at Resa. "Dammit!" he screamed again.

During the prior months tempers had flared between the two—over insignificant things like lab space and equipment. At some point, they began to question each other's role in a project on which both were working. Friction had finally escalated to all-out violence.

I pulled Resa aside. "What's wrong with you, for crying out loud?" I asked him, becoming angry myself over the incident.

Resa spun around and retreated to Guo's lab across the hall, where he sat alone at the bench, staring at one of his research logs.

Volker burst out another door into the hallway, where he stood in the middle of the floor, screaming in German. It sounded like World War II was about to start again.

145

It was pointless trying to calm him down. My college German was no match for whatever was spewing through his agitated lips.

I chose to join Resa instead, closing the door to the lab as I entered. Outside, Volker's ranting died down to a muffled commotion, punctuated by the loud smashes of breaking glass.

"Resa, this is ridiculous," I said. "You guys are two of the best researchers here. No one would believe this."

"He's crazy," Resa said, still staring at his research log. "I don't know what's wrong with him."

"That's not the point."

"What is the point?"

"Look, Resa. The point is that we still have to finish our work no matter what."

"Well the 'what' is already upon us."

I knew exactly what Resa was talking about. It was strange, but no one in the department had ever discussed openly what they really thought about the accusations that had accumulated against Gallo. We all had busied ourselves with the continued struggle to conquer this deadly and frightening disease. If any of us had any doubts about his explanations of the rapidly accumulating evidence against him, it was never discussed amongst us, never discussed between more than two people in the hearing of others.

Although neither Resa nor myself stated the obvious, we both were thinking the same thoughts. Things just didn't fit.

In January 1983 the group at the Pasteur Institute had prepared a tissue culture of a lymph gland from a patient with many of the problems my patient, Gary, had. They demonstrated the presence of an enzyme needed by the virus to replicate. But they had difficulty maintaining the tissue culture. Gallo suggested adding a second type of blood cell to the tissue culture.

In February 1983 the group in France sent a batch of blood specimens from their lab to Gallo. Using the technique suggested to the French group, he was able to demonstrate the presence of strange viral particles by magnified pictures of infected blood. Gallo later stated that the lab was not able to isolate this virus. Not long afterwards, the French group published their paper demonstrating evidence that patients with AIDS probably had an infection, and that this infection was probably the new virus shown in their article.

In July 1983 the French group sent a suspension of their new virus to Gallo's lab. There was "not enough virus," Gallo later said.

In September 1983 one of the investigators in Gallo's lab pooled a collection of blood cells, blood fluid and a second batch of virus particles. This was used to infect uninfected blood cells in tissue culture. From this culture the AIDS virus was isolated. To distinguish it from the virus previously isolated by the French group, it was given the name HTLV-III.

In May of 1984, a flurry of papers from Gallo's lab appeared in the journal *Science*, essentially demonstrating to the world that this virus was the cause of AIDS.

The proclamation of this discovery was so monumental that it leaked from a journalist—informed by Gallo of the event—before it was officially printed in one of our scientific journals. The news exploded onto the front page of the Sunday *New York Times* on April 22, 1984. As a result, the Secretary of Health, Margaret Heckler, forced Gallo to make an announcement.

History followed.

When the U.S. Government filed a patent for the HIV test, based on Gallo's virus, the French group began to sense that something was amiss. They immediately claimed that this virus was in fact theirs, sent to Gallo during the prior year.

The basis for denial of this claim has been that the French virus had not been isolated from the specimens sent to the lab.

When the AIDS virus' genes were later sequenced, they were found to be essentially the same as the virus first isolated by the French.

The world was told that somehow the viral culture used to isolate the AIDS virus was contaminated by one of the specimens sent there from France.

For those of us in the lab, the issue became one of intent versus enthusiastic carelessness. It really didn't matter which of these possibilities was true since the result was the same.

The investigation of the lab's discovery of the AIDS virus escalated. Our society has a tenacious opinion about the role of truth when it comes to matters of scientific investigation. If we, as scientists, do not seek the truth, as expressed by God in the laws of nature, then the value of our endeavors is nonexistent. But more than this, if we are incapable of reassuring the public of our honest intentions, then we have lost the battle for knowledge before it is fought. The justification for our pursuits becomes insignificant.

The fact that our society devotes such a significant amount of resources to science and research affirms its expectations. As a consequence, our society is understandably impatient when it comes to matters of its health. It expects science and research to produce truthful outcomes and to achieve this by an honest, fair effort.

Unfortunately, this is the reality of *society's expectations*; sometimes it is not the reality of the grueling, competitive world of research. Betrayers of the truth in science have always existed: Galileo exaggerated the outcome of some of his experiments; Isaac Newton decided to use a "fudge" factor to increase the predictability of his magnificent theories, as though their beauty was not enough; Johann Bernoulli, a lover of calculus, decided to steal his own son's equation, calling it his own; many of John Dalton's experiments allowing him to develop his atomic theory can't even be repeated by others; Gregor Mendel, the father of genetics, produced statistical results that are still too good to be true; even Admiral Perry wasn't at the North Pole when he said he was, when he knew he was still hundreds of miles away. At least his untruth was understandable; it was probably just too cold to convince the rest of the foolish world that he had accomplished the impossible.

I dislike Paul Broca's foolishness most of all. He managed to convince the world that human intelligence was based on brain volume. As expected, he adjusted the results of his measurements to his liking when evaluating the skull of certain races. But when his brain was later displayed after death, it was found to be pitifully small—not much bigger than a large monkey, to be exact. Fitting.

Such devilishness was ignored by the scientific community until 1981, when Al Gore, an unknown congressman, pressed the president of the

National Academy of Sciences to account for some of the recent, out-landish, falsified research that kept showing up in places like Harvard and Yale.

The response: "grossly exaggerated." It was a way of telling congress to mind its own business.

In a short four years later, such deceitfulness had become the whole world's business. And my business. The problem is that scientists are human; but then, I have known since childhood that we humans are "slightly" less than perfect.

It became my business because it was the flaw that could destroy the goal representing all that I had achieved in life, the flaw that could bend my shoulders for the first time—shoulders already burdened with the weight of a difficult beginning. My anger was explosive.

How could anyone choose to place oneself in an advantaged position when everything in their life had been at least a little more fair? How could one do such a thing at the expense of someone else's worthy efforts? How could one ignore one's own integrity?

I could not attribute my questioning fury to simplicity. After all, I knew the realities of life all too well—Cabrini's teachings are unforgettable, and life's ugliness had been made perfectly clear to me. The anger that I felt was primordial, a relic from battles fought long ago. It was the kind of anger that would set my mother in a flailing rage when one of her children was threatened. It was the kind of anger that never seemed to rupture outward through my father's breast, turning instead inward and destroying all of his substance. It was then that I realized what I had already known as a child. Much of life's unfairness is the offspring of the selfishness of others.

But with that small naivete remaining, I still found it hard to believe that anyone in the most visible research institution in the world, performing historical research, would behave in such a haphazard way, forcing the world to come to the conclusion that a little lie was told to cover an untruth. And if a little lie had been told, it would become the greatest deception in scientific research this century—maybe ever, as far as I was concerned.

The troubled waters that had seeped into my life in the lab swelled and then overflowed into the outside life I had been ignoring. My wife had become pregnant again, after having a miscarriage. Somewhere along the way I had set aside the non-expedient — the things I thought could take care of themselves. During that time, my wife had become weary with the way of things in Washington and with the thing she seemed to understand the least — her husband, who he was and where he was heading in life. Our existence together had evolved into periods of brief "hellos" and "good-byes". This was so despite the presence of my seven-year-old daughter.

Whenever we did find time to talk, the topic was the same.

"They're talking about Gallo on the news again," she would say cynically.

My own weariness was magnified by late night trips back to the lab and grueling hours spent at the bench. Then another concern crept into the recesses of my subconscious. Reports were beginning to appear indicating a real risk for laboratory investigators working with the virus. I remember one time opening the top of a high-speed centrifuge I was using and finding test tubes containing virus-infected cells smashed into shards of skin-piercing glass. While removing the broken pieces, one of my hands scraped across a sharp surface.

Moments later I plunged my unbruised hand into a vat of bleach and scrubbed the skin for nearly thirty minutes.

It was not the possibility of death that disturbed me. It was the way this virus destroyed human beings.

This was a time of emotional turmoil; it was a time of tense anger; and it was a time of disappointment, despite my achievements. Fortunately, although I was now a Research Associate, I still had the responsibilities of a clinical oncologist at the Institute. Although my interaction with patients had decreased over the prior two years, the short time I spent in the clinic reminded me increasingly that I was first a doctor. And the suffering of those I saw there reminded me of the importance of also being a healer.

Our second child was born in the spring of '87. Three weeks later my wife decided that she wanted to return to school.

"How are you going to do that?" I asked her as I sat in a chair holding my new daughter.

"Any way I can," she said, turning away.

"I know things have been difficult for you," I said, concerned, "but there's no way we can afford a baby sitter."

My wife's face remained stern, unmoved, unfeeling. "Then I'm going back to St. Louis where my family is."

I looked down at my three-week-old daughter and my heart broke. Of all the possible ways life could harm me, it had chosen the most devastating. I had already had too many losses in life.

Angela and I had been married ten years, and still we had not had a real chance to secure our commitment. My "calling" was always in the way. That tenuous bond had already been frayed by my exhausting Residency training and by her medical problems. Although she was a nurse, I never really felt that she understood what it was like to follow the path I had taken from Cabrini. And although she had admirable fortitude, I always sensed in her a lack of the fervor needed to understand the unseen things that make life the way it is. But what bothered me the most was the fact that my new daughter was only three months old.

Since it was I who had uncompromisingly uprooted the family in the first place, I decided that I had no choice but to let her and my daughters go back to St. Louis. I would join them later.

I wrote a letter to Gallo, explaining why I was leaving the lab. But deep inside, I knew that any respect he may have had for me could not cover the anger that rose in my heart. The thin film of truth in this world is already much too inadequate.

When I first stepped into Gallo's laboratory, he was already a National Institutes of Health world-famous AIDS researcher. Four years later, one of his scientists was convicted of a felony, his deputy director was indicted for embezzlement, he was accused of "stealing" the AIDS virus, and the promise of a Nobel Prize had vanished into mist in front of him.

Chapter Fourteen

I saw faces in the snow.

They all started out different, those faces—some smiling, some laughing, some singing—but they all ended up becoming the same face, the same sad face I had looked down upon as a child.

The undertaker hadn't tried to make my Uncle Larry look sad—far from it. He'd used his considerable skill to create an expression of contentment on that familiar face, an expression of eternal satisfaction.

Looking out my office window so many years later, I wondered if the undertaker had really believed that even his skills were sufficient to have made up for the bullet hole in the middle of my uncle's forehead, the one that showed the real truth of my uncle's final expression.

"Doctor Willis?"

"Yes?" I said, quickly turning from the window and the phantasmagoric scene in the swirling snow.

"Are you all right?" my nurse asked.

"Yes, thank you. I'm fine." I took the medical chart she extended.

"Mrs. Shannon is in Examination Room Two," she said, still looking at me with a concerned expression.

"Thank you."

Before looking at the file, I turned once again and gazed out at the snow. Just snow now, no more faces.

Winter had been hard on St. Louis that year, and the mounds of snow piled beneath my office window seemed to draw me toward stifled memories of my youth during Chicago's angry winters. Bitter as those memories were, they could be a sanctuary from the sufferings of my patients. Time mellows.

Mrs. Shannon was young. Too young to have to answer to the kinds of questions we cancer doctors are forced to ask in the face of life-shortening disease. Death, it seems, always stalks those too young.

I knocked on the door to the examination room and then stepped in.

"Hi, Doc!" Mrs. Shannon said, her face breaking into a wide, unrestrained smile.

"Hello, Mrs. Shannon," I said, trying to match her enthusiasm. Even as I did, I noted how gaunt she was and how her drooping shoulders confessed to a weariness that her spirited greeting couldn't mask. "How are you feeling today?"

"Great," she said. "I feel great. This is my husband."

I turned and faced the young man seated on the edge of his chair in the far corner of the examination room. He glanced up and nodded his head before returning his gaze to the shining tiles on the floor. He needed a shave and his uncombed hair hung to his shoulders.

His eyes held the terror that Mrs. Shannon refused to acknowledge.

I had carefully reviewed Mrs. Shannon's medical history and x-rays. Several weeks earlier, she had gone to her doctor complaining of a persistent cough, difficulty swallowing and a dull ache in the middle of her chest. He had prescribed antibiotics but they had done nothing to improve her symptoms.

A chest x-ray had shown too many shadows in the middle of her chest. A computer assisted x-ray brought the mass into clear focus—it ascended from the upper edge of her heart, spread along her windpipe and surrounded one of the large veins that drained blood from her right arm back to her heart.

I was now well versed in the nuance of cancer and had come to respect its cruel cunning. Her mass had chosen its haven chillingly well—here, it could be devastating and ruthless.

A thoracic surgeon had performed a biopsy by making a small incision at the top of her breastbone and slipping a hollow metal rod behind her sternum. When he turned on the light, he was greeted by a cancer so angry-looking under the microscope that it was impossible to determine if it had originated in her chest or if it had claimed this sanctuary from somewhere else months earlier.

153

"Any changes?" I asked her as I gently palpated the mass above her right collarbone.

"Sometimes I get a little more tired," she said, shrugging her shoulders.

Other than her thin frame, the only outward betrayal of her deadly enemy was the stony mass I manipulated with my fingertips.

"So, what's the verdict?" she asked, still maintaining a remarkable cheerfulness.

"Mrs. Shannon, because of the location and position of your cancer, there is no way for it to be removed surgically. I'm afraid I'm going to have to admit you to the hospital so you can undergo chemotherapy." I watched her expression. Her eyes were riveted on me, but her expression did not change. "You're going to require radiation treatments as well.

"It's the only way we can do any good."

"Anything you say," she said. "Together, we're going to lick this thing."

I appreciated her determination. No one as sick as she was got better without a strong determination to do so. "It's not good, Mrs. Shannon," I said.

But I did take small solace in her confidence. I looked over to her husband, still sitting with his head facing the floor. He began to shake his head slowly.

"Why?"

I waited a moment. "Why what, Mr. Shannon?"

He looked up at me and the rims of his eyes were red. "Why didn't they find this months ago when she first started coughing? Why did it take so long?"

"I can't answer that, Mr. Shannon. A cough could be a symptom of so many things . . ."

"Are you sure then?" he asked, leaning forward. "Are you sure of what this is?"

I nodded. "Mr. Shannon, I'm as sure as the lung doctor and the chest surgeon who sent you both to me."

I turned back to his wife. "It's not going to be easy for you, Mrs. Shannon. I won't even know if we're doing any good until I get you through at least two sessions of chemotherapy."

"When do you want me in the hospital?"

"Yesterday," I replied.

Her smile faded and a look of bewilderment replaced her expression of resolve.

"I was just kidding, Mrs. Shannon."

Her smile returned and she sighed, a deep, relieved sigh. "I'm glad you have a sense of humor after all. For a while there I thought you were taking this worse than me."

"I'll admit you to the hospital tomorrow," I said.

Mr. Shannon slowly rose from his chair. "I'm sorry if I was rude before," he whispered, extending his hand. "These past few weeks have been awfully hard. You know?"

"I know," I assured him.

"Would it be all right if our little boy came in to see her? He's only five . . ." He was out the door before I had a chance to reply.

The look on Mrs. Shannon's face reflected her husband's pain. She seemed to allow herself to suffer only within the context of his anguish.

"I do understand," I said to her before she left.

My nurse had already slipped the medical chart of my last patient of the day into the rack on the door of another examination room. I looked at the name. Julius. My lips formed a tight line.

Only three weeks ago, Julius felt a dull ache tugging at the muscles of his right groin. That ache crept down into his testicle, where his doctor discovered an uncompromising lump crowding the space in his sac. When he came to me, Julius had just been discharged from the hospital following surgery to remove the tumor—and the testicle.

I slipped the chest x-ray out from its envelope and clipped it to the fluorescent screen outside the examination room. I flipped on the light, already knowing what I was going to see. I was hoping that somehow all the egg-shaped masses strewn across the dark shadow of his lungs had somehow disappeared while the x-ray resided in the envelope.

I quietly entered the room. Julius was at the window, his back to me. His broad, proud shoulders sagged slightly as he watched the snow swirling down from the sky.

TO WALK IN MY SHOES

His sullen face, haloed by a full head of frizzy hair—reminiscent of the Afros of the 1960s—was reflected in the frosted glass of the window. I waited a few moments before violating the sanctuary of whatever peace he'd been able to discover since his world had been turned upside down less than a month earlier.

There was something in his stance and expression, looking out at the snow, that stirred me, that reminded me of someone else . . .

"Hello, Julius, how's it going?"

He did not answer right away. His eyes moved slowly along the street below the window before he turned from the window and faced me. A brief, uncertain smile animated his lips. His eyes glanced at me, then quickly away. "I'm not sure, Doc. Maybe you can tell me."

I felt a familiar sadness come over me. Taking care of Mrs. Shannon was going to be difficult. For different reasons, getting Julius through his illness was going to be equally hard. Mrs. Shannon's cancer was going to be the determined enemy in our battle together. For Julius, there were other enemies, enemies fighting a guerrilla war within his own soul.

I could see it in his eyes, his disquieting, doubting eyes.

Years of taking care of the dying had taught me well. There was always a clue. The tone of voice. The lack of enthusiasm in their greeting. The incessant tears. The gaze that avoided contact. The anger.

Julius had that anger. I could see it as he waited for my answer. There were never enough answers — just as there had not been for my mother those many years before, at the inquest of my uncle's death. And no matter how carefully chosen or how carefully worded, the answer that I had for him was unacceptable.

"Let me have a quick look at you, Julius," I said.

He sat up on the examination table and docilely accepted the press of my hands above his collarbone as I searched for swollen glands. He breathed deeply on command as I listened to his lungs through my stethoscope. He lay down as I palpated for masses in his stomach. He endured my examination of his incision stoically.

This examination was a wordless attempt on my part to establish trust. A glance at Julius' blood test results told me what his chest x-ray had already made clear. Certain cancers produce proteins that spill into the blood.

The cancer marker in Julius' blood was ten thousand times the normal level.

"Well?" he asked when I indicated he should sit up.

"Julius," I said, "we have a problem. It's going to be okay though," I added quickly. "The cancer has—"

He narrowed those angry, suspicious eyes. "Has what?"

"It's gone into your lungs, son," I said softly. I knew that no matter what I said or how I said it, he would hear my words as a death sentence.

He slid off the examination table and returned to the window. He remained silent. However, I could see his reflection clearly in the glass, and I saw the first tear slide down his cheek. Finally, he nodded his head in resignation.

"Julius, we can cure only about five types of cancer. Yours is one of them."

His head shifted as if he'd snorted in disbelief. "Come on. Who you kiddin'? You just told me I got this stuff all over my lungs . . ." Then, his defiant anger dissipated. "It ain't fair. It just ain't fair."

"Julius, the odds are overwhelmingly in your favor. The medicines we use for your type of cancer have been very successful.

"There is a good chance I can get your tumor into remission, and a reasonable chance that I can cure you. Son," I added, "I have every intention of doing precisely that."

I couldn't be sure that he heard what I was telling him. He continued with his soft protestation that it wasn't fair. "Just when I thought I was going to catch a break." He turned and looked at me. "I just got a job. Somebody finally gave me a chance and this . . . this had to happen."

"Son, I'm going to take care of you," I said. My voice was urgent, and I wasn't sure if I was saying what I was saying more for his benefit or mine. I knew the current chemotherapy for testicular cancer was very effective, and yet . . .

Perhaps it was the strength of Julius' sense of unfairness that was seeping into my thoughts, germinating, growing along with seeds long ago planted, growing with the strength to undermine my determination. "Have you spoken with your family?" I asked him.

"All I got is my mama. My father left a long time ago."

His words seemed to cut at me. I breathed in deeply to control my voice. "You've got to call her. Ask her to call me. Please. I need to admit you to the hospital in the morning to start your treatments."

His grip on the windowsill was tight. The tension in his fingers extended through his hands and up his forearms. He waited several seconds before he spoke, when he did, there was a curious resignation in his voice.

"It's like someone's playin' this bad joke on me," he said. "I made it through high school when everybody else I knew didn't. I did good in woodshop class. But every time I tried to get into one of those construction training programs, I'd end up doin' nothing but pickin' up the garbage around the construction site.

"But I watched and I listened and I learned a lot. I'd go home and find a neighbor who needed work on his house and I'd do the work. I got good," he said, his voice firm with pride. "Real good. After a while, they started askin' me for my help at the construction site. Man, I made them all look like all they had was thumbs," he chuckled.

"I bet you did, Julius."

"One day, the big boss come onto the site and he saw me working. I gotta tell you, I was sawin' and hammerin' and nailin' like Noah on the Ark, so this boss man asked me how far along I was in the trainin' program. When I told him I ain't even started yet, his mouth fell open.

"You know what?" he asked, turning from the window and looking at me. "He hired me on the spot." But his confidence quickly evaporated again. "And now this."

Then I recognized the feeling that had been growing in my thoughts, that had been pressing against my sternum and sending pain and sadness deep into my chest. Then I knew the faces that I'd seen in the snow—the faces that had all become one.

I knew them well.

I knew Julius' face. Just as I had known the face of my Uncle Larry, sad and worried even in death. Just as I had known the face of my Uncle Robert, accidentally stabbed to death by my aunt during yet another one of his drunken quarrels; as I had known it on my best friend's twelve-year-old brother, murdered by a bullet fired by a gang member; as I had known it on my first patient, dying in spite of my determined efforts.

I knew this face and the deep sadness residing behind its eyes, masked only by the anger and suspicion burning in them.

I had known this face when I said goodbye to my father in his hospital room, and then a week later, as he lay in his felt-covered, plywood coffin. I had known this face on the faces of my brothers as they eased my mother's pale, sky-blue coffin into the ground.

I knew this face too well. I would have known it on my twenty-four-year-old brother, Steven, who died alone in a cold, dilapidated room in a Chicago boarding house after I returned to St. Louis.

No, I told myself, I would not let Julius die. Despite my own beginnings, I had endured. I had been made stronger by the pain, by the ceaseless expression on that face, that face I was beginning to recognize as my own whenever I glanced at the mirror. I had used that pain as fuel to flame the fires of my own desire and determination in life.

Unlike so many others, I had endured to reach a place where I could prevent the life-ending harm Julius' cancer intended to inflict upon his twenty-four-year-old soul. I could prevent it. And I would.

"Julius," I said, my voice filled with quiet, determined fire, "Julius, I am going to help you. I will not let you die."

He looked at me with a slightly confused expression, as if the very hope that I held out so determinedly, the very hope that he longed for, was the one thing that most troubled him.

Futility, once planted and taken root, is a fecund and overwhelming emotion.

The following day I admitted Julius to the hospital.

At odd times—in crowded rooms, in elevators, alone in my office—I find myself looking down at my feet, half expecting them to be the same, "wrong" feet of my youth. Seeing that they have become the straight and true feet of an adult causes me some momentary confusion, as if I cannot quite comprehend the path they have tread from those long-ago days to now.

At these times, I find myself thrust into a kind of engulfing silence—

a deathly silence—one that dominates regardless of the sounds and voices around me. Then, after a moment or two—I don't really know how long—a single note begins to fill the silence, a note I recognize as well as I recognize any sound on this earth.

This note is clear and pure. It opposes the isolation and the confusion that roils within my being. Then another note joins the first. And another after that. I know these notes as well as I know the voice that sings them.

It is the voice of my mother. My mother, making her music.

When she wasn't somehow making music, those silences were among the most frightening memories I hold of my childhood.

Silences belonged to my father.

Music belonged to my mother.

To hear my mother chant was to hear the sound of angels singing at the throne of God. Melodious, churchly ballads or soaring choruses. Depending on the state of her soul, her chant could be the whisper of a reverent refrain. It didn't matter. Whether she was anguished or joyous, her music carried with it the hope and promise of grace.

While listening to the lilting beauty of my mother's voice, I could often decipher the events unfolding in my family. From her lips came messages of wisdom and guidance beyond the music itself.

Sometimes I would hum one of the melodies my mother sang while I studied the x-rays of a patient. There, lost in the images of my patient's life-and-death battle, I would find a moment of grace, a calmness that let me stare unblinkingly at their struggle and, sometimes, see in it my own, different struggle.

"What was that you were humming?" Mrs. Shannon asked me one day.

I had come to know Mrs. Shannon well during the period that I treated her. Her unbound cheerfulness was deep and sincere. It reached to the very core of her being. Her hopefulness and cheerfulness battled against the demons of doubt and pain which managed, on occasion, to sneak into her life.

Her mother had always known that her daughter was an optimist. Her husband had learned early in their marriage that, for his wife, the glass was never half full; it was always completely full, even if to his eyes it was empty.

What I knew better than either of them was that the enthusiasm that grew out from her being was sometimes the difference between life and death for cancer patients. Her spark of fervor could make the difference in surmounting the insurmountable.

It was her zeal that was so uplifting. I recognized in her passion the embers of other, long ago sparks in my own life. This I cherished in both of our beings.

"Just a song my mother used to hum," I explained to her as I took the films down from the lighted panel.

"Do you know the name of it?" she asked, leaning forward on the examination table.

I shook my head. "No." Then I paused. "It's funny. I can't remember the name to a single song my mother sang. I don't even know if they were specific songs so much as melodies."

Mrs. Shannon was nodding. "My mother used to hum all the time."

When I had admitted her into the hospital, even with a whole night to consider what we had discussed in my office, her eyes still glowed with fire and determination.

I never soften the reality of the difficulty of the treatment I provide for my patients. It is not an easy road. But Mrs. Shannon remained cheerful and ready in spite of a night to sleep—or not sleep—on the knowledge of what the next few weeks would bring.

For four days, there was little music for Mrs. Shannon. Her time passed in a blur of needle sticks, x-rays and intravenous medicines designed to keep her from vomiting relentlessly.

Two weeks after being discharged from the hospital, she was readmitted with a high fever and a white blood cell count close to zero.

"What's happening to her?" her husband asked me when I came to see her.

"This is the price we pay to give her a chance," I said, comforting both him and myself.

Fortunately, Mrs. Shannon's second cycle of chemotherapy was much kinder to her than the first.

"Okay," I said to myself as I pulled the films from the envelope five weeks after we'd started.

I took a deep breath. Although I knew there had to be some emotional distance between my patients and myself, this was always a difficult moment for me—a very difficult moment. In the privacy of the x-ray viewing room, I was the first to see if I was, indeed, a healer.

I snapped several views of her chest scan into place on the illuminated x-ray viewing box.

The mass that had engulfed the middle of her chest had collapsed on itself, leaving behind stringy, tenacious tendrils that still clung at anything nearby.

Her response was good. We were on our way.

Mrs. Shannon brought her five-year-old son to her first check-up. She had gained several pounds and her x-rays looked good. Even Mr. Shannon was in good spirits. But the child was frightened. He couldn't shake the fear within himself.

Midway through the check-up, as her son clutched her arm, Mrs. Shannon tilted her head down and began to hum to him. A calm seemed to come over him as she continued to hum.

I was entranced by her gentle, lilting voice. It took several seconds before I realized that the melody that she hummed to calm her young son was the very melody I had been humming several weeks earlier while studying her x-rays.

In my mind, I heard her gentle voice grow bolder—fuller—until I heard my own mother again, humming the melodies. They played over and over in an endless loop, carrying with them the images of my youth.

Chapter Fifteen

After I left NIH, I often thought of the things that might have been. However, I did complete my task in the laboratory. I left it up to Resa to organize and analyze the data that we both toiled to produce. He published some of the results a year after I had gone back to St. Louis. A couple of years after that, Resa went back to Iran.

Gallo survived the onslaught. He later became the Director of the Institute for Human Virology in Baltimore.

Although I had left the laboratory, I had attained my goal. I was alone on the mountaintop of my own making. From there, I could look around and see the valleys and canyons, the smaller peaks and the difficult paths that had made up my life.

From that vantage, I began the process of assessing my life. I was no longer the sum of the things I could accomplish. It was time for me to look back and try to understand the significance of my life's substance. It was time for me to try to understand who I was, so that I could better understand who I had become—and who I might still become.

The process was not an easy one. Indeed, in many ways it was more demanding than the arduous and painful one that had led me through life. Things had gotten back on track. I had joined my wife a year after she returned to St. Louis. We had, again, accepted the unspoken knowledge that our union had a purpose. That it was this to which we needed to cling in order to survive all that had happened and all that would happen during our marriage.

For a time, turning within did little to reveal the true "me" to myself. One evening, as I sat quietly reflecting in my study, my wife came in and sat across from me.

"It's time," she said.

I looked at her curiously. "Time?"

She nodded. "Time to go back."

I wasn't sure I understood what she was talking about.

"It's time to go back to Chicago."

The calmness of my face masked the tug-of-war of emotions hidden beneath the surface of my faint smile. I hadn't been back since . . . since my mother's funeral. I didn't want to go back. Not to Chicago. I wanted to leave that place behind.

But Angela was right. How could I understand myself—or help my two daughters understand me, and therefore themselves—if I did not return at least once?

I dreaded the journey. But the following spring, with my wife and my daughters, I drove back to Chicago.

Our hotel room was on the third floor. When my wife opened the curtains of the windows, we could see that some of them overlooked the rooftop of the hotel lobby. The roof was bounded on three sides by an unusual positioning of the hotel's walls, allowing access only from the front of the building, and only by the use of a two-story ladder. However, because of the strange configuration of the hotel, our windows were only a few feet from the rooftop.

My five-year-old daughter called me to one of the windows not long after we arrived.

"Hey, Daddy! Look! A bird!" she said, pointing jubilantly out the window.

He was huddled in a corner, in a patch of debris he had painstakingly gathered to make a shoddy nest. His thin, weathered, dull feathers stood on end each time a gust of rain-laden wind swept its way into the cove. Nearby lay a tiny pile of breadcrumbs and leaves, which he had apparently hoarded for food.

"Daddy, what's he doing there?" my daughter asked with her nose plastered against the windowpane. "You think he flew there or something?"

As though in response to my daughter's question, he slowly lifted himself from his nest and began to make his way to a puddle of water, where he began to drink.

164

That is when I saw his lifeless, broken leg. It dangled from beneath his frail body, useless.

At that moment another gust of wind blew into the cove, followed by pounding rain. He lifted his body once more and hopped to the far side of the cove, to the protection of the steep walls that rose above him.

"Daddy, is he going to be all right?" she asked anxiously.

I worried for him as well, so much that I tried to open the window to go onto the roof, but it was permanently sealed.

"I hope so," I said. For my little girl's sake, I then slowly closed the curtain, hoping that he would continue to survive as he already had, with a determination that seemed to be ingrained.

There, on that lonely, isolated rooftop, unknown to the world around him, he was learning how to fly again.

The following day the rain stopped and a flood of sunlight warmed the roof and the cove, but the sparrow was gone. We didn't know what to think.

Had he been swept away by the storm?

Had he soared off into the sky?

That morning I stole away from my family and drove west, inland, on Lake Street, to that part of the city which does not exist for Chicago's torrent of springtime visitors. Lake Street carried me past the drab, red brick frames of the Henry Horner projects — now towering stacks of stone, still struggling to remain upright after thirty years. I stopped briefly to let the roaring screech of the L-train dissipate overhead into the distance.

With an effort, I retrieved from memory the sight of Horner's lush red bricks and the wooden planks leading to unformed breezeways. For a moment, the echoing laughter of a seven-year-old child, as he bounced up and down on the wobbly shafts of wood, reverberated in the recesses of my memory. Then the rushing roar of another L-train overhead jolted me back to the present.

Carefully, cautiously, I ventured further down Lake Street, further into my past. Instinctively I turned down a narrow side street.

Suddenly, I realized that I had been there before. I was engulfed by a deluge of memories: the tingling chill of winter wind against my skin;

the soft glide of a sled's metal blades over caressing mounds of cottony snow; the snap of a rope against a rusty, red kerosene can, teetering on the sled's back; the plaintive whisper of a little boy's voice.

I stopped my car in the middle of the street. What lay before me was little more than a patchwork of vacant lots and scattered, worn bungalows. Nothing defining. Nothing identifiable. There, in the middle of the block—where a two story brick building had once stood, wedged between a factory and a white frame house—was only a clearing covered with small piles of bricks.

But the absence of things did not stay the memories. The clamor of a fire truck careening around the corner in a cloud of powdered snow. The flaming orange and yellow smoke spewing from the windows of a building. A stream of water suddenly stopping in its path and turning into a patch of ice. A woman's voice, pleading for comfort. The disappearance of the kaleidoscopic, red and white lights of an ambulance into a curtain of feathered snow.

I lingered there until all the memories faded away, until they were sequestered again into their eternal dwelling places. Then I drove back out to Lake Street and headed east.

I was surprised at how easy it was to find Odgen Avenue. It was now blocked off by a row of concrete slabs. I drove around the barricade and followed Odgen's path for several blocks, to the point where it began to soar upward toward Cabrini-Green.

The dingy, gray shadows of Cabrini rose—one at a time—into view as Odgen climbed higher and higher. When I reached its peak, I suddenly stopped. From there I could see the cluster of Greyhound buses lined in their stalls below me... in the bus station to which my mother and I had come every Sunday on our way to Mantino to visit Uncle Larry.

A patch of grass lay at the bottom of Odgen's descent. Stanton Park's sparse acreage was unchanged. Although the pitcher's mound had been long lost in the sea of encroaching weeds, the bench where my father often sat near home plate was still there, still paying homage to the quiet man who once dreamed there.

I cautiously got out of my car and stood at a distance from the entrance to the building where I once lived. I lingered long enough to get the attention of a muscular young black man sitting on an upturned wooden crate, not far from where I now stood. He had been watching when I first pulled up. I knew the look in his eyes well. It was the defensive, attentive stare that forewarned its recipient of possible danger. In Cabrini, it was immediately evident to me that things had not changed. Only faces had changed. The instinct for survival seemed to have passed on to each new generation.

I slowly strolled over to where he sat.

"How goes it?" I asked, as friendly as I could.

"You know, man," he said, looking at me with a softening of his fiery stare, "just hangin' in there."

"My name's Rudolph."

"They call me Pee Wee," he said, with the hint of a smile. "You don't look like you live around here."

"I grew up here," I said, pointing to apartment 112, at the end of the building. "Twenty-five years ago."

"Man, I wasn't even born then," Pee Wee said, finally smiling.

"Yeah, that was a long time ago," I said, taking a seat next to him on the grass.

"Well, what you doin' here now?" he asked.

"I don't know," I said, suddenly realizing that we were sitting right across the street from where the tavern that my uncle had walked into a long time ago once stood. "I just had to come back for a moment."

"Man, you show must have a good reason for comin' back to this place," Pee Wee said with a distant look in his eyes. "I'd give my life to get outta here," he added after a long silence.

We were both silent for a while, each lost in his own reverie.

"I know what you mean," I finally said. "But I've found out that although you may not live here anymore, this place will live in you wherever you live."

Pee Wee glanced at me in disbelief. For him, the thought of leaving Cabrini and still having to carry a part of it with you would probably be too terrible a price to pay.

We talked for a long time. I was wrong. Cabrini was not the same. It was worse. Pee Wee told me how the Disciple gang had taken over most of Cabrini, to control the flow of drugs in the area. As if to support his statement, gunshots rang out among the buildings every now and then while we sat talking. I told him about my days there: James' and my crazy brotherhood, the other terrors of death, how good blues sounds played late into the night on a guitar, and the joy he will feel if he doesn't give up and one day walks away from Cabrini-Green.

"Take care of yourself," I said before leaving.

"You too, man," Pee Wee said, nodding his head with the kind of motion that affirmed our unseen bond.

For some reason, after leaving Cabrini, the image of the sparrow returned to me while taking my family to the Shedd Aquarium for lunch. There, we sat at a table next to a huge window that overlooked the aquamarine waters of Lake Michigan.

Suddenly a shadow appeared, high above the frothy waters. It hovered, swooped, then soared to an even greater height, where its magnificent white-tipped wings rode the wind.

It was a seagull, strong, bold and free.

My thoughts immediately traced their way back to the rooftop at the hotel. I wanted so much to believe that the sparrow had made it, that he too was free.

I squinted up into the bright sky again, at the marvelous sight high above, and smiled at the thought of the small, crippled sparrow in flight. Then I realized that I was like the seagull also, because I no longer needed to learn how to walk through the difficulties in this life. I, too, had proven that I could soar.

Chapter Sixteen

When I returned to St. Louis, I met with Mr. and Mrs. Shannon to review her course. They were grateful for the good news I was able to give them. The x-rays continued to show improvement.

"We still have a long way to go," I told him. "But we're in a good place now."

Cancer treatment is a very capricious process. Some cancers seem willing — almost glad — to relinquish their grip on patients. Others are more tenacious. If they are left with a single foothold, they will grow again — quickly, angrily. If they are denied the foothold they will find a way to hide somewhere else, establishing a new sanctuary. They can be relentless.

"We may have a ways to go, but we're going to do it," Mr. Shannon said.

I had never seen him sounding so hopeful. In the past, he had struggled to show a brave face for his wife's sake. I had no trouble imagining the difficult times he suffered when he was not in her presence.

On the other hand, Mrs. Shannon went through her entire chemotherapy without once losing hope. Her courage was never forced; her optimism was never hollow.

She had become a beacon in the oncology ward, helping others look for the bright side in spite of the horrors of their diseases.

The staff felt a particular warmth toward her and so were especially glad to learn that the treatment seemed to be helping. They all knew how hard each and every patient's death could be. If Mrs. Shannon were to lose her battle to cancer, they would all feel the loss.

I marveled at her inner strength, and working so closely with her, I knew her attitude to be the outward face of inner strength and not of denial.

"How does she do it?" my nurse asked me.

I simply shrugged my shoulders. "I don't know," I admitted. In that admission, I was stating a truth about myself. I cannot — and have never been able to—fully explain what it is that really allowed me to rise above where I came from.

Just as I cannot explain why now, while I live in a world so far removed from the world of my youth, my heart still cries out for those days so unrelentingly.

Three months after Mrs. Shannon had completed her treatments, she returned to my office.

"How have you been?" I asked her when I came into the examination room. I knew from the chart that she had come to see me because of a cough that lingered longer than it should have.

"I just have this cough," she said, interrupted by the self-same cough. "See what I mean?"

I nodded. "How long have you had the cough?" I asked her as I placed my stethoscope against her chest.

Although there was some deep congestion, which caused me concern, she had not been losing any weight — always a good sign.

"Let's take an x-ray so we can see what's going on," I told her.

A short time later, I was facing the x-ray in my office and wondering how I would explain to her what was so evident on the film before me. Her mass had returned.

"Dammit," I whispered to myself.

"I wish I had better news," I said honestly as I came back into the examination room.

"It can't be that bad," she told me.

"The mass has come back, Mrs. Shannon," I said, gently, directly.

She was quiet for a moment. "So, do I have more treatments then?"

"I have to be honest with you. This is not good."

"It's going to be okay. I know it will."

"The treatments won't be easy," I told her.

"I never asked for it to be easy," she said, smiling.

That was true. Never once had I heard her ask for anything other than a chance. I was determined to give her one. I admitted her to the hospital, where she received a continuous, massive dose of chemotherapy, all the while being subjected to daily radiation treatments.

In six weeks, I had shrunk the mass in her chest to little more than a faint shadow.

Her husband was grateful for the progress, but he was wary now. He had become a veteran of false hopes. In spite of the shrinking of her tumor, Mrs. Shannon was little more than a wisp of a person. The treatment that she had undergone was relentless and toxic, taking its toll on her body.

I had developed a great admiration for Mrs. Shannon. She faced the most tenacious of adversaries, determined to overcome. Unfortunately, her cancer was equally tenacious, equally determined. The cancer continued to lurk within the remaining faint shadows in her lungs. Quietly. For a few weeks. A month. A season. Spring faded into summer, which gave way to another frigid winter.

Then it began to grow. This time, it grew steadily and mercilessly, crowding out the space needed for her airway.

I could no longer treat her in my office. I had to admit her to the hospital one last time in order to care for her. But now my task was different. There was no hope that I could fight the cancer that had overcome her defenses.

Now I hoped to give her the one thing I believed that she deserved above everything else—dignity and relief during her last days in this world.

She was treated not like a patient, but like a guest by the staff, who had come to know and love her.

On a cold November evening, Mrs. Shannon died while her husband cradled her head in his arms.

The world is not, I am afraid, a fair place. My history knows that, and precious few of the things that I have done to try to put distance between myself and my history have been successful in undoing that unfairness.

Chapter Seventeen

There was no music in Julius' voice when he had sat opposite me in my office. No, in Julius it was all fear, unspoken and unbearable. He had every right to be afraid. He had not lived long enough to learn how to prepare himself for death.

"I'm going to help you," I promised him — promised him for all the ones that were gone before I was able to help.

"Doc, this is my mother," Julius said the next time he came to the office.

"Hello," I said, extending my hand to hers.

"Hello," she said, quietly. It was not her voice, nor her touch, nor her physical presence that was like my own mother's; it was her eyes, which had the same fierce determination — and the fear that her determination would not be enough to save her son. I had often seen these in my own mother's eyes.

In truth, his mother looked nearly as young as he did. But her eyes, her eyes were as old as any mother's who has ever breathed. She held him closely while I answered her questions about the treatment for his cancer.

"The cancer has metastasized to his lungs," I said at one point.

Silence greeted this statement. After several moments, Julius raised his head and looked directly at me. "Am I gonna die?"

My reply was quick, determined, and honest. "No, Julius. Not if I can help it."

After admitting him to the hospital, I flooded his body with intravenous fluids. This was done to prevent the metallic chemotherapy he received from destroying his kidneys.

"I almost did it," he said proudly when he was ready to go home, nine days later.

I looked at him curiously. "Almost did what, Julius?"

He smiled. "Almost made it without throwing up. I really tried not to throw up."

He *had* done incredibly well, vomiting only twice during the entire treatment.

I expected to see good things when, after two sessions of chemotherapy, the time came to review his x-rays. I had every reason to be hopeful. The tumor marker measured in his blood had already disappeared. Even so, I stood for several seconds at the view box in the radiology department before I began to flip the scans of his chest and stomach onto the brightly-lit panels.

My eyes moved down the outside of the folder, where the radiologist usually jots down his initial impression. In tiny letters he had written "better."

I quickly snapped one film after the other into place.

The softball-sized masses in Julius' lungs had completely disappeared. There was nothing on the film but heart, vessels and chest wall. It wasn't "better." It was gone.

But when I looked at the stomach scans, there was something still sitting there, nestled in the back of his abdomen where huge, swollen lymph glands used to be.

I was not alarmed. Patients with bulky testicular cancer often have small residual masses left behind after their initial chemotherapy.

Julius would require more chemotherapy.

However, after two more sessions of chemotherapy, the small mass on his abdominal scan was still there.

"I have to recommend surgery," I told him. "That's the only way we can find out what we're dealing with."

Julius lowered his head. I watched the tears drop from his eyes and stain the legs of his trousers. As far as he was concerned, I had given him a death sentence.

And if my chemotherapy had left any cancer behind, he would probably have been right.

"I don't know," he said finally, struggling to contain his emotions. "I don't know."

It took several office visits before I was able to convince him to have the surgery.

I was with him when he woke up in the recovery room. His eyes immediately sought mine.

"The mass was benign," I said, patting his shoulder.

This time when he cried, he was crying tears of joy.

Not long ago, Julius came to my office with his four-year-old son for his routine check-up. He is still in remission, seven years after that surgery.

I thought a great deal about Julius as I left my office that day and went out to my car to drive home. I remain determined to help all of my patients, but this determination has in itself over the years resurrected so many splintered images within my soul—images powerful and fleeting, like the snow flakes that fell all around my car. I felt somehow disconnected from myself.

As I drove through the swirling snow, the images went deeper than my patients' expressions of sadness and pain. I visualized fleeting images of my childhood, of innocence and playfulness. There was Uncle Larry, alive and animated with laughter. There was Uncle Robert.

Then I drove eastward, toward the paling rays of the sun, into the darkening evening.

Past the lighted sanctuaries huddling the western shore of Lake Michigan, where the Windy City still rises up like a flame against the bitter winter of my memories.

Afterword

My life churns on, for now. Each of us would like to reach a point in this existence where we simply know all that has gone before has some meaning, some significance. Any of us could probably offer up some tidbit of understanding and guidance to others just starting along what may be formidable paths, paths that may lead to some minor greatness or oblivion.

I have, thus far, survived life's impediments. I have looked for no excuses, no causes, and no blames. Perhaps this has been easy for me because of an unrelenting faith, and an overwhelming inherent sense of my own ability—graciously granted—untouched, unmoved, unhindered, and unstained by a world filled with ignorance, hatred, jealousy and selfishness.

But what does this mean for others who may be like me? Too few survive the kind of roots from which some of us spring; too many fade away, like Henry, Paul, Forest and Ken. Any one of them could have altered all of our lives in an historical way had the social fabric in which they attempted to exist been different. Been kinder? Been more supportive? Been justly due?

The advice I have to offer our "gifted" children—some huddling at this very moment amidst poverty-strewn surroundings—goes beyond a praise of their intelligence. It is for all of our children:

First, you are who you were intended to be, chosen by your Creator to be everything that you truly are—valuable, teachable, and capable without end. You are not what others think you are, or what they may want you to become to satisfy their own sense of worth and stability.

If you are to fulfill your God given destiny, become disciplined early, despite your surroundings. Be prudent in the choices you make when your peers urge you down a deadly, drug-infested, violent, wasted path. Drugs kill the mind, soul, and body. This truth will never change. If you ignore it, no hardship and no one on this earth can be blamed for your inevitable downfall.

Always do what is right and just, for your sake and others. Although others will always exist who do not understand this spiritual law, you must not let their evil ruin what life still has to offer.

Never belittle the value of family. Look around you. The wasted lives caused by bad living, destructive environments, and indecent acts reflect the destruction of your heritage. Show esteem for what parents, brothers, and sisters you may have left. In a moment this could change.

Apply yourself wholeheartedly to all that you do. Remember, even the mediocre becomes more noticeable when done with perfection. Sooner or later your labor will produce the goal to which you cling.

Bad company inevitably produces bad results. If you run with a violent crowd, it's easy for violence to find you. If you have seen enough children die, you will eventually understand this. Dying is not easy, not easy for anyone. I know, I've seen enough. Besides, your violence is the justification for keeping you constrained, a justification for denying you access to the privileges of society.

Respect all that is respectable. But remember, everyone has worth—even those who place obstacles in your way.

Choose your role models carefully. Ask yourself, "have this person's acts touched the lives of others in a way that has made those lives both more tolerable and more fulfilling?" If not, look elsewhere.

If you are a child and you produce a child, it does not matter if it is a result of a foolish choice, an accident, ignorance, or moral deprivation. Blaming your poverty or society does not change the result. You now have two mouths to feed. And society has already made it quite clear that it will not do this for you. Why bring another soul into this world to suffer want?

Finally, honor what intellectual gift you may have. Do this by seeking your education with a passion. It is priceless. Never forget that the greatest harm done to you in this life will often come from those who are ignorant of your worth. A sharp, educated mind will do much to help you maneuver around the walls that you will inevitably face.

There is no such thing as a racist society. Only the individual who has learned how to be a bigot exists. His or her preconceived notions, based on ignorance, unjustified fears, and misconceptions of superiority allow the lumping of masses of human beings into one category for convenience. There are few people more unique than the ones you have met here. They are real. They have minds, bodies and souls that have sometimes paid dearly as the result of the acts of harmful people, people who then blend back into that nebulous haven—society. They disappear back into the commonality of their own lives, never having been held accountable for that one act that may have deprived someone else of a job, a place to live, an education, or simply a chance.

Although these individuals may not be the majority, the amplification of their deeds continues to tarnish the greatness of our country. But more than this, it burdens the decent hearts of others with a guilt they should not have. And it has plunged a whole race of people into a cesspool of insecurity and paranoia. The toll for all of us cannot be repaid for generations. You see, the sons are still paying for the sins of their fathers. Yet, we should not forget that the sins of the fathers become the sins of the sons, if they choose to reaffirm these sins by continuing the attitudes, acts, and beliefs of those before them. Why should any of us burden ourselves with staid, old beliefs that are simply and patently untrue? Beliefs that continue to belittle us in the eyes of the Third World. The fact is that it is easier for *individuals* to elevate themselves to moral greatness than it is for a nation. But if enough individuals do so, then their nation becomes great.

My few words add little to the reams already written about the racial demon that gives America no rest. Like many, I can offer no immediate solution, none that is useful for "society" as a whole. It is only useful for a single person. That same person will inevitably show accountability for all of his or her life, because like all of us, he or she will surely die and return to the dust from which we all came.

Poverty weighs heavily on America. It is not a child unique to our soil. It has existed among humans every since one group decided that "more is better." It has existed for eons. On countless continents, it has existed. And it has existed in countless societies. What pales America's gleaming skylines is its existence in the most prosperous nation in modern times. That very prosperity sways the beams of the bright lights in the direction of Detroit, Chicago, Los Angeles, New York and Appalachia, ferreting out the answer to the question "why does this exist at all?"

Poverty exists because we are who we are. Some have, and others have less. Some have most, and others have none. This basic fact seems almost simplistically idiotic when you hear it verbalized. But what is not simplistic is how things got to be the way they are, and why they do not change—and may never change—if we continue to attempt to fix the problems the way we have in the past. Jesus once said, "you will have the poor with you always." This was a reflection of His understanding of human nature. He knew, too well, the human tendency to take care of self, and self only—even when there are ample resources for others. Given the opportunity, humans seem to always prefer superiority of participation and opportunity at the expense of others. That this phenomenon occurs across racial, cultural, and religious lines is evident. We only need to look at India's caste system, Africa's tribal upheavals, and the heinous history of South Africa.

Lost or prevented opportunities have devastating, cumulative effects. The overwhelming majority of poor people in this country did not get that way by choice. Most people do not *choose* to suffer. The cycle of forced deprivation, poor educational opportunities, and exclusion is a vicious, heartless cycle. And it is fueled by an individual who decides not to approve a loan, offer a job, or sell a house to another, solely because that person is "not like me" or "the people I know". These single, individual acts—relentlessly performed—can and have decimated the full potential of generations of African-Americans and others. The result is a mass of poorly educated, ill-equipped, hapless souls who are now looked upon with disdain. The disenfranchised condition is then seen as justification for more abuse.

God is just.

It is for this reason that we all will be held accountable for our acts in this life. The system can no longer be blamed. It is no longer the problem. And it no longer requires fixing.

It is clear. You cannot legislate compassion and fairness into harsh hearts. They can be changed, sometimes, by enlightenment. I hope that these words are just a beginning.

Finally, a word to my colleagues, who also attempt to heal human beings. It has been said that "only the hurt physician can heal." Obviously, many of us do a remarkable job repairing broken bodies. But this is too often done with a cold heart. Human beings are much more than the flesh we attempt to revive. And more often than not, it is a broken spirit that causes us to lose the battle. Remember this. And remember that you, too, will probably become a patient someday. If so, hope that the one caring for you knows how to help you die by applying the compassion you may have denied others.